DISCUSSION-BASED ONLINE TEACHING TO

ENHANCE STUDENT LEARNING

DISCUSSION-BASED ONLINE TEACHING TO ENHANCE STUDENT LEARNING

Theory, Practice, and Assessment

Dr. Tisha Bender

STERLING, VIRGINIA

Published in 2003 by

Stylus Publishing, LLC
22883 Quicksilver Drive
Sterling, Virginia 20166

**Library of Congress
Cataloging-in-Publication Data**
Bender, Tisha, 1953–
    Discussion-based online teaching to
        enhance student learning: theory, practice,
        and assessment / Tisha Bender.—1st ed.
        p. cm.
    Includes bibliographical references (p. 197)
        and index.
    ISBN 1-57922-065-7 (alk. paper)
    1. Internet in higher education—Social
    aspects. 2. Online Education, Higher—
    Computer-assisted instruction—Social
    aspects. I. Title.

LB1044.87.B43 2003
378.1'734—dc21
2003005083

To Nicky

CONTENTS

PART II   PRACTICAL APPLICATIONS

PART III   ASSESSMENT

ACKNOWLEDGMENTS

Writing a book is like producing a play; it involves the coordination of many actors and technicians, all of whom make a vital and significant contribution. Although some play larger parts than others, all are equally important to the harmony of the final production, and so I thank them all most warmly and sincerely.

My warmest thanks and gratitude go to Dr. Stephanie Nickerson, a person of extraordinary generosity, who thinks about promoting the good of others, and ceaselessly opens doors for them. From Stephanie I have received suggestions, comments, sources, and encouragement. I am also grateful to Mona Kreaden, who was willing to take the risk to try something completely new and different, by employing me to train interested NYU faculty to teach online. Also at NYU, I thank Dr. Ken Bain, who has a great interest in fine teaching; Vincent Doogan for his generosity and commitment; Jeff Lane and Keith Adams, both of whom have that rare combination of technical expertise, and knowledge and understanding of teaching; and Lucy Norris and Emma Rossi, for always being pleasant and helpful. My thanks especially to all the NYU online instructors with whom I have worked, and in particular to Dr. Kathy Hull, Dr. Diane Grodney, Dr. David Hoover, and Dr. Bapanaiah Penugonda.

At Cornell University, School of Industrial and Labor Relations, I wish to sincerely thank Dr. Carol Robbins, who believes in me and has given me many wonderful opportunities to teach online and train others to do so, too. Her encouragement and generosity have been an enormous help. I also thank Holli Broadfoot for her steadfast technical skills and dependability, Bev Brown for her benevolence and terrific sense of fun, Irma Hernandez for always being kind and generous, Vanessa Figueroa for her pleasantness and dependability, as well as Gordon McClelland and Lisa Mattes, in Albany, with whom I have always had great online and phone discussions.

I would also like to thank my editor and publisher, John von Knorring, for his clearheaded, exciting, and challenging suggestions, and for his civility and promptness in responding to me at all times.

Finally, I would like to sincerely thank my friends and family. Special thanks to Dr. Sharon Packer, for her encouragement and generosity, especially that day in Woodstock, Dr. Gerda Lederer for her interest and enthusiasm, and to Dr. Lori Rosenberg, who is a character of unfailing patience and kindness, and who helps in immeasurable ways. I also give my heartfelt thanks to my parents, who were my first teachers and fine teachers in their own right, and who established in me the love of teaching; to Billy, Nigel, Joanna, and Tim for their encouragement and their humor; and most of all, to Charlie for his technical wizardry that surpasses all others, and Jonathan and Jeremy for their interest, intelligent input, and patience. And of course, this acknowledgment cannot be complete without also thanking Homer for those wonderful daily walks, on which my mind was refreshed and free to formulate thoughts for this book, and to J. S. Bach, for the beautiful musical accompaniments while I worked.

INTRODUCTION

> The reasonable man adapts himself to
> the world: the unreasonable one per-
> sists in trying to adapt the world to him-
> self. Therefore all progress depends on
> the unreasonable man.
> —*Shaw, B., 1983,*
> *Man and Superman*
> *(The Revolutionist Handbook)*

Reasonable or not, those of us who embark on online teaching do so because we want to do something that is educationally progressive, is innovative and beneficial, and adds an extra dimension to the courses taught on campus. The rapid diffusion of computer acquisition and Internet access is well known, and online education is snowballing. How quickly we take what is innovative, and heap each new paradigm shift onto our grateful laps. But, without careful deliberation and intentional focus on the needs to understand pedagogy, as it unfurls online, we run the risk of producing a cohort of students who pass through the educational process, missing out on true opportunities for inspirational and meaningful learning, and for whom the online class might amount to little more than knowing where to click within a labyrinth of links.

The specific purpose of this book is to switch emphasis from the technical issues of online teaching to the *human* implications of teaching and learning by communicating through the Internet. It aims to investigate the thinking behind the technology, why we use it, and how we can make it effective for our needs. Online pedagogy is in its infancy. In the campus class, we generally know what works well, such as the importance of speaking sufficiently loudly, writing clearly on the board, being dynamic, maintaining eye contact with students, and inviting students to take an active role in discussion. But what works well online? It is the discovery of the most effective online teaching methods that is the focus of this book.

Discussion-based online education is primarily text based. It is also asynchronous in nature, meaning that all online participants can log on and participate in discussions at a time convenient to them. This can present new intellectual challenges, but it can also make education accessible in innovative and exciting ways. Online discussion can reach beyond the temporal and spatial constraints of the campus class, and as a result can often add a richer and deeper perspective as students respond when they are informed and inspired.

There are many reasons accounting for the growing popularity of online classes. Faculty and students appreciate and benefit from the convenience and flexibility of online education, and enjoy not having to spend the time or money traveling to class. Administrators are glad that online education alleviates any shortage of classroom space, which is an important concern as the population continues to grow, and there is increasing popularity in continuing education and lifelong learning. Many educators also feel that learning how to learn in an online course is becoming a necessity, and will equip students with a skill they will continue to need throughout their lives.

There are two alternative ways in which the Internet is used in online teaching. One is that the entire class is held online, and the students and instructor do not see each other face to face. This literally opens up global possibilities for learning, and students from across the country, as well as around the world, might log in to study in these classes. Students from New York, London, Mexico City, a traveling dance company, or a boat moored off the Florida coast, for example, can communicate with each other, with the instructor, and with the guest lecturer from India, by a simple flick of the switch. Besides being tremendously exciting, it can also be very enriching for students to learn from others from different cultures, and it can help to break down cultural barriers.

The other way in which the Internet is used in teaching is when a class which meets on campus, has an additional Web component, and this type of class is called a "hybrid". Some educators consider the hybrid to be the best of both worlds, as it facilitates the learning process and enhances both student–student and faculty–student communication. It provides the convenience and flexibility of the asynchronous online method of learning, with the real time face-to-face contact. We are all familiar with the situation of being immersed in a terrific discussion in the campus class, and then having to stop as it is the end of the scheduled class time. Rather than having to wait for the next campus class, by which time the idea might have lost some of its force, the discussion can continue online. In this way, the hybrid class can be thought of as "pushing back the classroom walls." As well as continuing discussions after class, the online environment can be used for preparation of materials for the next campus class. This has the added advantage that it can assist in identifying any areas of difficulty.

Another advantage of the hybrid class is that different learning styles and methods can be accommodated. For example, some students might be shy or reluctant to speak in front of a group on campus, yet open up more freely when in front of their computer screen, and the reverse might be true for other students. Some students do not learn well from lectures, and many students actually discover their own voice for the first time when working online. Furthermore, providing the means of communicating information through a variety of media and environments might help students to be able to engage in more class activities than if it was solely one type of environmental forum. As Dennis Pearl, a professor of statistics at Ohio State says, "You can make the best roast beef that you can, but a vegetarian is not going to have a good meal. I think the best model is to provide a really good buffet" (quoted in Young, 2002b).

A third advantage is that the different phases of learning can occur in different environments, which has important implications on instructional design. Kolb's (1984) Learning Cycle suggests that there is a continuous cycle of four processes when learning takes place: experience, reflection, conceptualization, and planning. The campus class might be the most suitable environment for gaining an experience (such as watching a film, seeing an exhibit, or hearing a reading) and possibly might also be the best place for planning, whereas sandwiched in between, the online class, due to its asynchronous environment, might be the most appropriate forum for reflection and conceptualization.

It should be pointed out that all the remarks made in this book address online teaching in general, whether the class if fully online or a hybrid, and that the book will consist of three parts:

- Theory: an application of learning theories to online discussion-based courses
- Practice: suggestions and techniques, illustrated by real examples, for stimulating and managing online discussion effectively, and for improving online teaching practices
- Assessment: methods for assessing the efficacy of discussion-based online courses

PART I

THEORETICAL IMPLICATIONS: BUILDING A BODY OF ONLINE PEDAGOGY

This section is devoted to building a substantial body of online pedagogy. Much exists in the literature about pedagogy of campus teaching, but to date more needs to be discovered about the theory of teaching students who are remote from us, and with whom we communicate via online discussions. In an effort to better understand online pedagogy, the following topics will be investigated.

- The distance factor
- Optimal roles of the online teacher
- Rethinking learning theory as applied to online learning

I

THE DISTANCE FACTOR

Now, here, you see, it takes all the running you can do, to keep in the same
place. If you want to get somewhere
else, you must run at least twice as fast
as that!
—*Lewis Carroll, 1871, Through the
Looking Glass*

Can the Mind Exist Independently from the Body?

Students generally like to have a sense of belonging. When they attend a class on campus, they become familiar both with the room in which the class is held and with the regularity of attendance of the inhabitants in that room. There is, in other words, a sense of predictability in terms of environment. Feeling included in a group is an important factor for encouraging the true potential for learning to take place.

But is it possible for a class that does not occupy spatial coordinates to still generate a feeling of *place*? Given that students in an online class are working remotely, often some distance from each other, does the association of "distance" and "learning" constitute an oxymoron? After all, education is surely about the meeting of minds, not their separation.

Dreyfus (2001) criticizes the possibility of learning without physical presence, as is done via the Internet in online courses. His book, *On the Internet,* covers the "hype" of hyperlinks (as he does not think it leads to intelligent information retrieval), asks just how far distance learning is from education, talks of how a "telepresence" is necessarily disembodied and therefore inadequate, and explains how what he sees as the anonymity of virtual online discussions leads to loss of meaning (as stated by Arnone, 2001).

Dreyfus says that early philosophers such as Plato, and later the French philosopher Descartes, believed in the philosophy of dualism; namely, that the mind is self-sufficient and in fact better off without the body as it can transcend time and space. He disputes this view, however, instead preferring to think as Kierkegaard and other existentialists did, that the body plays a crucial role in the learning process, as real immersion in any situation—which, in itself involves taking risks—can only occur through the physical body. However, I believe that within education, risk is generally experienced more by the emotions than by the physical body, and as such there is as much risk taking in the online class as there is in the traditional class on campus. Students in either setting risk being wrong, risk feeling embarrassed in front of the group, and risk not working at the same pace as others. Maybe the feeling is experienced and perceived differently, but it is still there.

When we participate in an online class, where are our bodies? Our physical bodies are positioned in front of our computers, but our virtual bodies can be anywhere imagined. We indeed use this split between the physical and virtual body when we talk on the telephone. I would disagree with Dreyfus that this split makes us anonymous, because in the online class our responses are always posted with our names attached. But the fact that we have no physical presence, Dreyfus argues, means that any learning that occurs can only be intellectual, not pragmatic. In other words, it is more on an abstract plane than involving a grasping and mastery of particular skills. He thinks that true learning can only take place from physically being somewhere and doing a particular activity, and it is only under these conditions that information becomes relevant and people come to meaningfully understand reality. But if this is true, how can anyone learn anything from a book, newspaper, television, radio, a letter, or e-mail? Is not the expression of the content more important than the medium through which it is expressed?

Differentiating between Space and Place

Gertrude Stein, when looking about in Los Angeles, said, "There's no 'here,' here," and I think her words can be aptly applied to the online class. Perhaps, though, any confusion about the online class can be clarified by differentiating between the concepts of *space* and *place*. Robinson (2000, p. 112) defines space as "an abstract container determined by distance, direction and time." In addition, she says that place exists within space as a localized region. Place, as in a class, should be like a magnet, which holds together the instructor with a community of students and their ideas, knowledge, thoughts, and memories. In short, place is defined as anything that is mutually shared within, and has a boundary for, containment purposes (Robinson, 2000, p. 112).

But what of cyberspace? Because it is virtual, Robinson argues that it is "the world of imaginary tools, that produce art, poetry, literature . . ." But, pragmatically speaking, place within cyberspace is created and defined by the computer program, and its strictures of authorized access and passwords, which ensure that only those intended to belong to this place actually do so.

Since the online class is potentially interactive, this will involve the element of time as well as space. Robinson questions whether the words of her response are present for the students when they appear, or only when they are read. Is she, as instructor, imagined as present in her class only when her responses are posted? But, by analogy, do students in the campus class that meets at discrete intervals only think of the instructor as present when the class actually meets? I believe that the main objective in either teaching environment is for the subject matter to be so inspirational, exciting, and challenging that students think about it beyond the time in class, whether on campus or online. In the online class, Robinson states, time becomes space, because all responses, though posted temporally, must be laid out spatially across the two-dimensional computer screen.

Distinguishing between Physical Distance and Transactional Distance

In an effort to further understand the impact on teaching and learning of students and the instructor working remotely from each other, I want to focus on one element within Robinson's definition of space, and that is the word *distance*. *Webster's New World Dictionary* (1990) offers the following definitions.

1. Being separated in space or time; remoteness
2. An interval between two points in space or time

3. A remoteness in behavior; reserve

4. A faraway place

I believe that computers with Internet access can give us potential ways of meeting, if not physically, then at least in the exchange of knowledge and ideas. In other words, it is not physical distance that is our concern, but the *relational* distance between teacher and student. In *Webster's* third definition of distance, we see something about remote relationships, but we as teachers certainly do not want to have a psychological remoteness between students and ourselves.

Michael G. Moore (1984), contemplating the meaning of distance in education, states: "There is now a distance between learner and teacher which is not merely geographic, but educational and psychological as well. It is a distance in the relationship of the two partners in the educational enterprise. It is a 'transactional distance.' "

How can this transactional distance between teacher and student be understood? Saba and Shearer (1994) suggest that this can be thought of as the relationship between the requisite structure for the teacher and the degree by which students take the initiative in their own learning. In other words, transactional distance is the extent to which the teacher manages to successfully engage the students in their learning. If students are disengaged and not stimulated into being active learners, there can be a vast transactional distance, whether the students are under the teacher's nose or on the other side of the city. But if a teacher, whether online or on campus, can establish meaningful educational opportunities, with the right degree of challenge and relevance, and can give students a feeling of responsibility for their own learning and a commitment to this process, then the transactional gap shrinks and no one feels remote from each other or from the source of learning.

Some critics of online education believe that it is deficient as it lacks physical presence along with the information of body language and tone of voice associated with it. But have we considered the large lecture on campus, in which the instructor might be unable to see clearly to the back of the lecture hall, let alone correctly read body language? Perhaps under these circumstances, very little besides obvious shuffling and student whisperings is even noticed. A reader's comment on Dreyfus's book, found on amazon.com, states: "I took one of Dreyfus's classes at Berkeley as an undergraduate and I never got to talk to him, there was no face to face learning." He went on to say how he had felt like a "disembodied presence" as an undergraduate, and how much more meaningfully interactive online classes were that he had subsequently taken.

On a similar note, in a somewhat tongue-in-cheek comment, Bromell (2002) claimed, "It's obvious, isn't it, that a pre-packaged distance-learning course that gives you a limited field of options to 'click' is more tailored to your needs than a trained teacher standing in the room with you, a person who can misread your expression and ineptly judge whether he or she is effectively communicating?"

I strongly believe that when students demonstrate commitment, it is to learning, knowledge, and the pursuit of new ideas; it is not commitment to a particular physical classroom, however lovely it may be. Therefore, I think that commitment to learning can take place without a physical setting, and certainly the online class can be effective as a virtual place to disseminate, collect, and exchange knowledge and ideas. In this way, then, it can be appreciated that physical distance and transactional distance are different measures, and whether a class is taught online or on campus, or a mixture of both, it seems that the goal is to minimize the transactional distance, thereby establishing a comfort level and ensuring ready access to fulfill all educational aspirations.

How the Social Dimension Impacts on Transactional Distance

Wegerif (1998) speaks of an important social dimension within online classes that will have a direct impact on transactional distance. In a fascinating study based on interviews with twenty-one students enrolled in an interactive online course at the Open University, Wegerif discovered that the degree of success or failure of students was closely related to whether each student felt like an insider or an outsider. Learning was therefore seen as a social process, as the degree of learning depends on whether there is a feeling of belonging to a community of practice.

One student remarked that what she had gained the most from the course was the collaboration with others, in which she learned an enormous amount from her peers and felt that great friendships blossomed between her and some of her online colleagues. Conversely, another student who had dropped the course before its end said she did not feel that collaboration could work well online, because unless she was prepared to log into the class every day, the conversations would continue without her, leaving her behind the pace and thus feeling overwhelmed.

This process, concludes Wegerif, is a social experience, as it is the difference between the student who crossed over a threshold into the position of fully participating in the midst of all discussions, and the one who did not, but who was left on the outside uncomfortably looking in. The student who felt immersed in this online activity was highly motivated, and could not wait to log back on to see what else was being said. The student who felt like an outsider experienced online learning as cold and remote.

An important study published by the National Research Council (2001), entitled *Knowing What Students Know: The Science and Design of Educational Assessment,* takes a similar view in stating that learning takes place in a social context. Collaboration is vital to learning so that students understand questions, develop arguments, and share meaning and conclusions among a community of learners. Knowledge, the National Research Council states, is not incorporeal or disembodied, but is developed through working with others. Although the study focused on grade-school children, their views are applicable to online learning as well, because even though working remotely, by interacting in online discussions, students establish an online community of learners, and through their exchange of written ideas their thinking becomes apparent to the instructor.

How did students in the online class studied by Wegerif cross the threshold? It seems it was a matter of confidence for some. For example, one student said that she initially felt like a novice hiding in the corner, and said very little until there was a particular group exercise, and since no one was contributing anything, she dared herself to offer her ideas. She received a very positive response, and from then on, felt she was able to fully participate.

Many other factors also affected whether students felt they had insider or outsider status. Access to the Internet, for example, had a big impact, as those who only had a computer at work and not at home were more limited, as were students who had significantly high phone charges for Internet hookup. Additionally, some students found it easier to write online than others, and for some it was quite frightening, especially if they felt unsure about a particular topic. Without a doubt, the medium itself had an impact on communication. One female student who worked in the so-called real world in a male-dominated environment where she was fairly quiet found that online she could respond more frequently as she had a chance to think things through and not be interrupted when she was ready to express herself. On the other hand, student postings of excessive length created disincentives for discussion, especially for students who did not log in frequently.

As Wegerif concludes, "Forming a sense of community, where people feel they will be treated sympathetically by their fellows, seems to be a necessary first step for collaborative learning. Without a feeling of community people are on their own, likely to be anxious, defensive and unwilling to take the risks involved in learning." Moving from the feeling of being an outsider to being an insider was central to achieving a positive learning experience.

These conclusions are validated by Diane Grodney (2001), a colleague who teaches hybrid classes at New York University. She stated, "I would frequently walk into my house, go to the computer and see if anyone was home. I shared this experience [with my class] as part of our ending process, and others said they strongly identified with the sense that we shared a home, a community or as one student put it, 'an educational holding environment' (a la Winnicott). Another student referred, earlier on, to the class as a transitional object which he/she was able to carry throughout the week. I believe these references speak to the sense of the personal psychological space that can be created online."

One factor that Wegerif does not address, but which seems crucial in attempting to decrease the transactional distance, is the behavior of the instructor, who, after all, sets the tone for the whole class. I believe that it will be beneficial for the instructor to personalize the educational approach as it will provide an important step toward compensating for any feeling of coldness or remoteness that messages on a computer screen might otherwise entail. This can be hard, not only because of class size, but also because of the diversity of students. Nevertheless, it is important to try.

The next section will explore in more depth the optimal role of the online teacher.

2

THE OPTIMAL ROLE OF THE
ONLINE TEACHER

> Passive acceptance of the teacher's
> wisdom is easy to most boys and girls.
> It involves no effort of independent
> thought, and seems rational because
> the teacher knows more than his pupils;
> it is moreover the way to win the favour
> of the teacher unless he is a very excep-
> tional man. Yet the habit of passive
> acceptance is a disastrous one later in
> life. It causes man to seek and to accept
> a leader, and to accept as a leader who-
> ever is established in that position.
> —*Bertrand Russell*

Who Do We Teach?

There is a much greater diversity within the student body than even a decade ago. It has been thought that typical college teaching methods were tailored to deliver content to white, middle class males, as they had traditionally been the dominant group. This group of individuals was thought in general to exhibit autonomous, competitive behavior, with an emphasis on achievement (Anderson and Adams, 1992). If this is indeed the case, then it calls for a need to diversify teaching methods, so as to pay attention to other learning styles.

Before exploring these ideas further, I would like to pause to question whether the assumptions of the white, male student learning style apply online. My experience, and the experience of many of my colleagues, is that whereas in the campus class, white middle class male students might have the most to say, and might even interrupt a female or minority student, such a thing is not possible online. (For a fuller discussion on the issues of gender and racial differences, see in Chapter 6, "How Do We Speak Online.") There can be no interruptions because the class that exists in cyberspace is equally available to all class participants at all times, nor is the online instructor able to favor specific students by looking primarily in their direction. Furthermore, traditional teaching methods that were designed to be most suited to the white, middle class male emphasized delivery of information in lengthy lectures; but online, there is the need for shorter, snappier mini-lectures, opening out into interactive discussion.

The Importance of Personalizing Education

We talked in the previous chapter about how an effective online teacher should try to personalize the educational approach so as to minimize the transactional distance. Certainly those instructors who are more attentive to individual students are more effective. Anderson and Adams (1992) mention that some students are "field-dependent learners," meaning that they are almost as concerned about the personality and style of the instructor as the course material that is being delivered. Factors possibly considered important in the instructor's style include being supportive and encouraging, giving ample feedback, being a good role model, being appropriately informal, and eliciting discussion. I firmly believe that these features can be perceived accurately online.

There are many different ways in which an instructor can be attentive to students, and this will depend on the role an instructor might take. McKeachie (1978) identifies six teaching roles for the campus teacher, all of which can be applied to online teaching. These roles can be used for different purposes and at different times in the semester. For example, the teacher can be seen as the following:

- A *facilitator* who enhances student learning by encouraging active participation in discussion and by helping the student to see education as meaningful and relevant. The instructor should resist having a condescending attitude toward the students, as if handing down information from a "celestial throne" (p. 253), but should be able to empathize with them and see the situation as they see it, by carefully listening to and learning from them.

- An *expert* who communicates expertise through lectures and discussions, and is able to stimulate students without overwhelming them.

- A *formal authority* who helps students by establishing boundaries such as acceptable conduct and dates of submission of materials.

- A *socializing agent* who has contacts within the larger academic community, and as such can be helpful to students in providing such things as letters of recommendation and links to research and publication sources.

- An *ego ideal* who is charismatic and shows commitment and enthusiasm not only to the subject matter but also to the students themselves.

- A *person* who demonstrates compassion and understanding of student needs.

Good teaching, I believe, is about modification and adjustment, in relation to the perceived needs of each individual student in the class at any time throughout the semester. McKeachie (1978) states: "Teaching should be a two-way process in which both students and teachers learn from one another; as long as teaching conditions facilitate two-way interaction, the good sense of teachers and students can be substantially relied upon" (p. 255). This means that the online teacher should be attentive to each student in the class, in an attempt to bring out the best in each of them. Now, bringing out the best in each student does not necessarily imply giving each of them loads of attention, or even the same type of attention, as some might do better with more responsibility for individual work. Just as a parent does not treat each child identically, but reacts to needs and personality traits of each, so too should the instructor do this with each student. It is all a question, therefore, of getting to know one's students.

Student Characteristics

McKeachie (1978) looks at various student characteristics, including independence and responsibility, authoritarianism, anxiety, intelligence, motivation, introversion–extroversion, gender, and cognitive style. Following are implications of these in terms of online teaching.

- *Independence and responsibility:* If insecure, a student will want more of a teacher's authoritative presence, whereas an independent student will want the teaching to be more permissive. I think the degree of independence can also be related to the learning activity. For example, in an online class of mine, I thought the students were articulate, highly motivated, and independent, as the discussion forums were positively explosive with their numerous responses. However, when I introduced a new activity of role-playing (see in Chapter 7, "Other Forms of Group Work") they became largely dumbfounded and in need of much direction and nurturing.

- *Authoritarianism:* Authoritarian students prefer a high degree of control, and listening to lectures. However, I feel that a hierarchical structure of this sort would not work well online, as lengthy online lectures by an overly authoritative online instructor might dissipate some of the energy of interactive online discussion.

- *Anxiety:* Because anxiety can be increased by uncertainty, it follows that anxious students do best in a highly structured environment. Anxiety can arise at different times in the semester, depending on the materials studied and the learning activities, so the online teacher must be encouraging, supportive, and prompt at supplying guidance.

I would like to mention at this point that the questions of independence and responsibility, authoritarianism, and anxiety are interrelated, especially over the decision that the teacher might make as to whether the class should be competitive or cooperative. If the teacher opts for collaboration, which works best in an online class within an online discussion, or could be continued through online collaborative projects and role-playing, this might also imply delegating more responsibility to the students themselves, which can cause anxiety for some. This might be because of the departure from an authoritarian, spoon-fed class, into one in which students are encouraged to think creatively.

As Kathleen Hull (2002), a colleague and instructor of a hybrid class at New York University, said, "Getting young people to think on their own and solve problems is inefficient, time consuming, and sometimes uncomfortable." But this, Hull concludes, provides the potential for a powerful learning experience for the students, and one that they are more likely to retain. I believe, too, if discomfort of this sort does arise, it is best for the online instructor not to supply the answers, but to be nurturing, encouraging, and available to student questions. It is in this way that online education is personalized and humanized. An interesting study conducted by the Higher Education Research Institute at UCLA in late 2002, which interviewed 32,840 full-time faculty in 358 colleges, found a significant increase (over findings in the base year of 1989) in faculty interest in students' well-being, and a commitment to helping students both academically and personally (Wilson, 2002). Although this study focused on campus teachers, the same sort of commitment is feasible for online teachers as well. The collaborative work could be balanced with independent work in which the student works alone offline by reading, researching, and writing papers. Together, independent and collaborative work can lead to greater learning and the development of critical-thinking skills.

- *Intelligence:* In the past, educators believed that a single intelligence test could measure whether a student was more or less intelligent. More recent thinking on the subject puts forward the view that there are multiple intelligences, and that students have diverse styles of learning and strengths in different areas. For example, some students might be visual learners; others intake information better if they hear it, or if they act it, or if they use their logical powers of reasoning. Howard Gardner, an influential thinker in this area, identified seven categories of intelligence, namely linguistic-verbal, logical-mathematical, visual-spatial, bodily-kinesthetic, musical-rhythmic, interpersonal, and intrapersonal. He then added existential, spiritual, and naturalistic (Gardner, 2000). Good teaching should therefore be cognizant of and tailored to the diversity of learners. How this can be carried out online will be the subject of much of this book.

- *Motivation:* To be a successful online learner, devoid of the peer pressure of the campus class, demands a high degree of self-reliance.

- *Introverts and extroverts:* McKeachie (1978) found that extroverts learn better when studying with another extrovert than when studying alone, and when performing original research. Introverts, in contrast, do better when directly fed information. Furthermore, extroverts care less for feedback than do introverts. It would be the subject of much fascinating research as to whether traits of introversion or extroversion are altered by communicating online as opposed to interacting face-to-face.

- *Gender:* McKeachie (1978) believed that female students were more concerned with achievement, and more willing to try to please the instructor, than were their male counterparts.

- *Cognitive style:* If a student is new to a subject area, or is predisposed to learning facts rather than application, greater personal contact with the instructor is preferable. This, though, depends on the type of interaction, the personalities of those involved, and the subject matter. I also would like to suggest that environment would make a significant difference, and if students do not see their instructor, as in the online class, they might feel that they need more frequent online contact than if they were on campus, irrespective of learning style. This might be especially true for students who are new to online learning.

The next chapter will look in more depth at the question of concept formation in an online class.

3

RETHINKING LEARNING THEORY WITHIN THE ONLINE CLASS

Some time ago, on a journey across the Atlantic, I reflected that the spoonful of mashed potato I was about to put in my mouth was actually traveling faster than a rifle bullet.
—*Edward de Bono, 1986,*
De Bono's Thinking Course

Hierarchy of Thoughts and Acquisition of Knowledge

The other day, a student in my online class wrote, "What do thoughts look like online? I mean, I know when someone is thinking when I see them, but online I only see the finished product of those thoughts." What a fascinating question! It points to how, in traditional, face-to-face education, so much emphasis is on the spoken word and on sensory cues that provide further information. But the advent of online learning speaks to a legitimate need to develop new teaching and learning paradigms, and to rethink learning theory within the online environment (Boettcher, 1999). This section will explore the impact that the primarily text-based environment of the online class has on a student's ability to learn.

John Dewey in his 1910 essay, "What Is Thought?," wrote of four levels of thought. First are the random, fleeting thoughts of which we are not particularly aware. For example, "I just heard a dog bark." The second level of thought is restricted to that which is not perceived by any of the five senses, so is more properly understood as thinking *about* something. The third level of thought is belief based, but these beliefs are unquestioned as they seem reasonably probable. The fourth level of thought is more reflective. These thoughts center on important conse-quences of particular beliefs, so it is important to provide evidence as to whether the initial belief is true. This implies that there is a level of doubt and uncertainty, which in turn stimulates an investigation. This fourth level of thought is therefore conscious and voluntary.

Assuming the reflective thinker is up to the challenge, what is the process of gaining knowledge? Dewey (1910) likens reflective thinking to a traveler being at a fork in the road; in other words, where there is ambiguity and a dilemma. The thinker, like the traveler, has to search for some facts and evidence to provide direction. Thus, thoughts can not exist in isolation from the real world.

Berge and Muilenburg (2002) also believe in a hierarchy of types of thoughts, culminating in reflective or "constructivist" thinking, which is constructing knowledge from personal experience. In addition, they iden-tify different types of thought leading to this stage, including critical thinking, which involves concept formation; higher level thinking, which is creative problem solving; and distributive thinking, which is shared thinking among the group. When there is collaboration and a sharing of personal experience between all class members, these shared multiple perspectives can lead to socially constructed meaning (Berge and Muilenburg, 2002; Wegerif, 1998; National Research Council, 2001).

Benjamin Bloom's Taxonomy

There is a definite need to enhance reflective thinking well beyond the simple acquisition of facts to be memorized, and to delegate more responsibility to students for their own learning. Benjamin Bloom pro-poses six developmental levels pertaining to the acquisition of knowl-edge and of intellectual analysis and skills (Cameson, Delpierre, and Masters, 2002). These are as follows:

• *Knowledge:* The lowest level of learning in the cognitive domain. It implies pure recall of memorized information.

• *Comprehension:* The second level of learning, and the first level of understanding. It could involve, for example, having the ability to translate words into graphics, interpreting the meaning of certain facts, or making predictions for the future. These can be achieved through discussion, either online or face to face.

- *Application:* The ability to meaningfully apply what has been learned to new situations. It involves a more sophisticated level of understanding than basic comprehension. Examples include solving mathematical problems, constructing charts, or applying theories to particular situations, such as in essays or role-playing.

- *Analysis:* Comprehension of the organizational principle of the material, so that it can be meaningfully broken down to its component parts, and the relationship between the parts can be understood. This is an even higher form of understanding than comprehension or application, as it involves understanding not only the content as a whole but also the constituent parts involved in its structure. Examples include understanding the structure of a creative piece of work such as writing, music, or art; identifying fallacies in assumptions; and distinguishing between facts and inferences.

- *Synthesis:* A higher level of understanding that refers to the ability to put what had been considered as disparate parts together to form a coherent whole. This might involve developing a new system of classification of facts or putting forward a research proposal. This is a creative process that endeavors to formulate a new structure for classification purposes; write a poem, story, or speech; or propose a scientific experiment.

- *Evaluation:* The highest area in the hierarchy of cognitive learning. It assumes all other areas and introduces value judgments based on defined criteria. The criteria can be internal, judging the organization of the work, or external, such as consideration of relevance; for example, judging the consistency of a piece of written work, the value of a work of art, or whether the conclusion of an experiment is supported by the data.

Paying Attention

If learning is based on experience, it would imply that a key ingredient in this is the ability and motivation to pay close attention (Levine, 2002; Fardouly, 2001). There can, of course, be various external stimuli that either increase or distract from potentially learning a new subject. If a subject seems relevant, meaningful, and exciting, then a student is likely to pay closer attention, although there is a diversity of learning styles, interest, and rate of comprehension. Students differ with respect to how they think, perceive, organize, remember, and solve problems. They differ also in their degree of interpersonal skills and level of independence, and whether they prefer active experimentation, reflection, or abstract concepts (Liu and Ginther, 1999). Ability to comprehend the language of the communication is another factor that will influence learning, so that if it is a second language or if the student has learning disabilities, this might interfere with attention span.

Levine (2002) identifies the following three categories that affect how we pay attention.

- *Mental energy control:* The body's ability to know when to concentrate and exert mental effort, and alternatively when to shut down at appropriate times, so as to rest or sleep.

- *Intake/processing:* The mind's ability to be selective, to know how to sort through a vast amount of data and choose what is relevant. It concerns establishing priorities and affects the ability to take good notes and develop good study habits.

- *Depth of information processing:* The mind's ability to incorporate information. The expression, "In one ear and out the other," would be a shallow incorporation of information, which is quickly forgotten. Some people, Levine says, naturally tend to see the broad picture, but nothing in much depth; and the reverse is true for others.

The Role of Long-Term Memory and Prior Knowledge

New developments in the field of cognitive science reveal that not only do conditions for optimal learning take place when a student is actively involved within a social context, but also that long-term memory plays a crucial role in one's ability to reason effectively about current information and problems. Short-term memory (also called working memory) is limited, so therefore it is best in learning situations for a student to evoke knowledge from long-term memory. As stated by the National Research Council (2001), it is of crucial importance to understand long-term memory, to see what students know, how they know it, and how they use that knowledge to answer questions, solve problems, and learn new information. It also helps to understand why certain situations seem relevant or meaningful to a student, and how a student organizes new information into manageable bundles or folders, termed *schema*. These schema imply that a student is sorting information into patterns which can be easily recognized, provide accessible storage for new information by making associations with something already known rather than being an isolated fact in a vacuum (Levine, 2002), and allow rapid retrieval of knowledge. It is through this storage of well-organized facts within long-term memory that a student can develop expertise in a subject area.

Prior learning, therefore, is of great importance and might assist students in learning new information. No one is a blank slate. When a student receives new information, he or she will reconcile it with what is already known in the long-term memory. This might lead to reevaluating or revisiting existing understanding, and the prior knowledge will help in judging the accuracy of the new information received (National Research Council, 2001). If the new information is judged to be accurate, it will be incorporated and thus knowledge in this area will be expanded.

Prior knowledge might unfortunately also cause some stickiness to old, incorrect ideas and unconscious resistance to change. For example, Ehrmann (1995) mentions that in the film, *A Private Universe,* during the commencement ceremony in Harvard Yard in the late 1980s, twenty-two graduating students, faculty, and alumni were asked why it is warmer in summer than winter, and why the moon has a different shape each night. Only two of those questioned provided the right answer, despite the fact that they should have been repeatedly given this information while in school. Ninth graders in a nearby school of good quality were then asked the same questions, and gave the same erroneous answers as those at Harvard. They were then taught about these scientific phenomena and asked the same questions again, yet clung to their preconceived notions despite having been taught the correct scientific explanations. It would seem, therefore, that during class time, the teacher asked canned questions and the students gave canned answers, while all along their preexisting theories remained invisible to the teacher and therefore unchallenged. This implies that even if teachers teach the right materials, it still might not impact on true learning, if the teacher remains unaware of the way students think. Enabling processes whereby student thinking becomes more visible to the teacher is of crucial importance, and will be studied in more depth in Chapter 9, which assesses the efficacy of online education.

Self-Regulating and Reinforcing Long-Term Memory

Since learning, therefore, seems so dependent on memory of what has already been learned, how do we ensure that we retain our memories accurately and do not become forgetful? The National Research Council states that if a student thinks about his or her thinking process, which is termed *metacognition,* this process of deliberation not only helps in self-regulation, understanding, and self-correction, but also assists in reinforcing long-term memory.

Levine (2002) also mentions that memory might be improved by transforming the information into a different representation. For example, if some information is given in words, then it could be transformed into a picture, or conversely a picture could be transformed into words. Furthermore, he states, memory will be influenced by time. If, for example, we learn one subject in one class, and quickly move on to the next class of a totally different subject, then it is possible that some information from the first class will be erased by the second.

When the acquisition of knowledge is brought about by directly experiencing the external environment, then the learner is thought to be active, as opposed to being a passive recipient of spoon-fed information. Fardouly (2001) breaks this process down into four steps: thinking about a new explanation, experimenting with it, experiencing what is occurring, and reflecting upon the process. Learning, Fardouly states, is an emotional process, but the right balance must be struck. Some excitement, encouragement, and challenge can be motivating, whereas too much anxiety over a course can severely limit the potential for learning.

Application of Learning Theories to the Online Environment

How can we apply these various theories of learning and knowledge acquisition to the online environment? Bruce (1998) poses the following questions.

- How does learning through technology serve in the development of experience?

- Is learning through the computer a substitute for other modes of learning?

- Is learning through technology in the same relation as a map is to its territory? If so, does this imply that it is not a real experience but a feeble abstraction?

- Conversely, can learning through technology give access to that which was previously inaccessible?

- Does learning through technology change knowledge?

- What is gained and what is lost as we move into the information age?

In an attempt to answer Bruce's questions, I first do not believe that technology is a substitute for other modes of learning, but that it forms a supplement to learning in the case of the hybrid class, or that it aims to produce a legitimate alternative in the case of the class held entirely online. However, quite how learning through technology serves in the development of experience is a question needing deep exploration. I think it is important to point out, though, that the computer is no more an experience than is the chalk an instructor might use to write on the board of the campus class. The computer is purely a tool of communication, in the discussion of experiences as related to education, and not the experience itself. In this way, I do not see technology in education as analogous to a map and its landscape as it is interactive and dynamic as opposed to being flat and static, and so I do not think in any way that it provides a "feeble abstraction."

Can Technology Give Access to Previously Inaccessible Information?

Bruce (1998) asks whether learning through technology can give access to information that was previously inaccessible, and I believe this can be so in certain circumstances. Technology, for example, can be invaluable in a course on meteorology, in which data could be retrieved on the Web of almost up-to-the-minute changes in temperature and wind conditions in any particular location around the world. On a different scale, an electronic simulation can show precisely in a matter of minutes how a flower grows, whereas in nature we might miss some steps in our passing observations (Turkle, 1995). But do we experience the flower the same way? No, I would argue that we do not; for we cannot bring all our senses to the flower, to feel its silky petals or drink in its fragrance. On the other hand, we might learn more about the growth of a flower through technology than firsthand observation, and as such, technology might well give access to that which was previously inaccessible. Perhaps if a Web site is of high quality, it might be of great immediacy and excitement, as sometimes technology enables us to experience things in a way that is larger than life. Thus, I would think that technology does change knowledge, but quite what is gained and what is lost is still to be determined and cannot be generalized.

Electronic simulations are but a small (or even nonexistent) part of discussion-based online learning, in which the technology provides a medium for the exchange of thoughts as well as the growth and development of knowledge. As such, the technology can all but disappear, as the focus shifts away from it, to the challenge of a good discussion in which the technology is merely the conduit. This permits Dewey's fourth level of thought, the reflective level, to occur.

Learning How to Use the Technology

By no means does the technology become immediately invisible. Any newcomer to an online class must first learn how to use the software. As with learning any new cognitive skill, initial use of the technology needed to access the online class will require effort, and will depend on the limitations of the short-term (working) memory (National Research Council, 2001). At first, the new online student or instructor will be very conscious of using the technology, and will have to talk his or her way through each step. It is only with continued use and positive feedback (meaning that the online user can access every part of the class immediately as desired) that familiarity with the technology will ensue, implying that both the skill and competence needed to obtain desired ends have moved into long-term memory. This will make the operation of the technology much more "fluent and automatic" (National Research Council, 2001, p. 85), because it no longer depends on the conscious monitoring of short-term memory used in the early days of the course. This freeing up of attention from the technology will permit the online user to focus on the course content, which after all, is the goal of the course.

Translating Concepts from the Real World to the Virtual World

The question remains as to how concepts, once formed through reflections about experience in the real world, are actually communicated in the virtual world of cyberspace? Do so-called relational learners (Anderson and Adams, 1992), who find relevance in the real world, place sufficient credence in the virtual world, the world of Web links and interesting and relevant online sites? Furthermore, in the campus class, we talk and listen; but online, the primary mode of communication is text based. When the online student reads the words of a lecture or discussion, that student co-constructs the meaning in a process that involves changing these symbols that appear on the screen into something meaningful by interpreting them in the light of experience. This is why, when any two people read the same material, they interpret it in different ways.

This highlights the tremendous importance of the *written word* in conveying meaning in the online class. Reading and writing, as opposed to speaking and listening, will no doubt have an impact on the way in which learning occurs, and the student who is a good text-based communicator will be at an advantage. Additional factors that will impact learning in the online class include the constant availability of every aspect of the course at any particular point in time, and the asynchronous nature of the communications.

Impact of Constant Information Availability and Asynchronicity on Mental Energy Control

This constant availability of information in the online class is in marked contrast to the campus class, in which once the session is over it is over, and is no longer available except through memory or notes taken. This continued availability of information online, combined with the asynchronicity of the environment, will impact greatly on what Levine (2002) has termed "mental energy control" (to know when to be alert and when to "shut down"), as it can allow for everyone to log on and participate when they are feeling inspired, and their concentration level is high and efficient. Conversely, it can be argued that the online class never goes away throughout the semester—there is no closing the door and imposing a limit, a boundary—so that there might be an artificial inducement for faculty and students alike, to get sucked in, to always feel the need to be there, even if they are beyond their normal limits of full concentration.

Impact of Constant Information Availability and Asynchronicity on Intake/Processing

Levine (2002) talks about the need for the student to be selective, establish priorities, and develop good study habits. But what happens in the online class, during which there is no need to take notes on a lecture, as all the information is available on the screen, all mini-lectures and discussions fully documented? What impact do so many words have on learning? I would like to speculate that it most certainly eradicates the need for memorization, but I think it absolutely challenges the need to be selective. Information can grow rapidly in the online class, and students will need to be shown which topics are of greatest significance, if they cannot determine this on their own.

It would be helpful to students, in terms of knowing how to be selective and properly establish priorities, if the course being taught is specific about its goals and objectives. In this way, students can gain a clear idea as to where they are going, and how topics are relevant within the larger context of the class (see Chapter 9). It has been found that chances for successful learning are greater when students are clear of the objectives, because then they know what is expected of them.

The pacing of the course, even an online asynchronous course, is important too, so that it is not so fast as to lose people, nor is it so slow that it makes some students frustrated (Fardouly, 2001). Furthermore, in a face-to-face class, students can often tell from the instructor's tone of voice which points are most important. Perhaps the best way to add emphasis in the online setting is to write the most important remarks in bold or colored text.

Impact of Constant Information Availability and Asynchronicity on the Depth of Processing of that Information and on Attention Spans

The question remains as to how deeply information is being processed (Levine, 2002). Does information presented primarily in written form make some people aware of details that they would normally overlook in a face-to-face context? I believe students have a great potential to absorb more information in the online setting, because they can take their time, work when they are at their best, and reread especially if they missed information through lack of concentration the first time. We might be learning at what Dewey labeled level-four reflective thoughts, but random level-one thoughts pop in and out of our minds, uncalled for and distracting: "I'm hungry," "Her hair looks nice today," "This evening I will iron my dress for the concert." One advantage of the online class over the campus class is that, if this occurs and we lose our concentration, the words are still in front of us on the screen, whereas on campus they would have evaporated into the air and become lost. Attention is more likely to be retained by a clear online course design and layout, with easy-to-find, meaningful sequences that have an inherent logic, and by short, succinct mini-lectures and discussion responses, rather than excessively long texts.

Tangentially related to this is that some claim we are teaching undergraduates who have grown up with short, snappy vignettes on *Sesame Street;* and that even in the popular culture, we hear truncated symphonies on the radio and read novels with shorter chapters and shorter total length (although there is a renaissance of public interest in lengthy novels such as *Lord of the Rings,* by J.R.R. Tolkien, and other epics). I believe that this is a reflection of social and cultural change, in which both children and adults often lead busy, overscheduled lives, possibly resulting in shortened attention spans. Also, the dominant influence of television and computer screens might encourage students to become visual learners, and point to the benefit of including graphics in the online classes. What is interesting to speculate upon, though, is the impact of seeing written text. Although the text is not a graphic, it is seen rather than heard. Quite possibly this has appeal to visual learners, by helping them to see the information rather than hear it, especially for students who have a photographic memory and can usually remember where certain words appear on the screen. Perhaps, contrary to the popular belief about the visual deprivation of the online class due to the lack of usual cues of the traditional classroom, there is for some people a different and incredibly effective visual component of seeing the written word.

Debate continues about how the Web has impacted on our concentration span. An article by the *BBC Sci/Tech News, 2002* entitled "Turning into Digital Goldfish," claims that most people click so rapidly through different Web sites, pausing only as much as nine seconds before clicking on to the next, that they have the attention span of a goldfish. This behavior indicates a feeling that the best is yet to come, that there is something just beyond reach and is ready to be discovered. This points to the need to design and facilitate an online class in such a way as to grab a student's attention, and retain it. Nik Halton's comment on the *BBC Sci/Tech News* interactive Web site is of particular interest: "I don't think the web is lowering concentration spans, just changing the nature of concentration used. With the ability to multi-task, looking at many sites at the same time, web users need to be able to hold parallel strands of narrative simultaneously, not just one. In this regard, it is no worse for concentration spans than a book or theatrical production which runs several plot lines concurrently." If this is indeed true, it has important implications for the online class, in which it might be possible to hold two discussion forums simultaneously, as well as other class activities such as visiting a relevant Web site or holding a group discussion in preparation for a presentation.

Information is likely to be more deeply processed and comprehension will be helped if, as in the traditional classroom, the most important information is repeated in different ways to accommodate different learning styles, not so that it feels boring and redundant, but so that it can be explored from different angles and truly comprehended. Boettcher (1999), for example, cites Stephen Hawking's book, *A Brief History of Time,* in which one reviewer commented that he knew what all the words actually meant individually, but in aggregate, he could not follow the text at all. Thus this reviewer could only see the symbols (words) representing the concept, yet had no access to the concept itself. To avoid an equivalent lack of comprehension about material taught in the online class, this might mean not only giving alternative written explanations, but also possibly inserting graphics or a sound or video clip where possible. A variety of learning activities also stimulates learning and helps to keep students attentive.

In the case of the hybrid class, students can log on to their computer after class to watch, read, or hear the class again, which may be useful to them if, in an effort to write it all down, they missed certain portions of the information. Despite the fact that some people worried that this online availability would encourage students to skip class, the rate of absenteeism was no higher in classes that adopted this than any other class on campus (Cabell, 1999). Some teachers of hybrid classes, however, prefer for the online component not to merely duplicate the campus class, but to enhance it by offering something more. For example, the same information taught on campus could be presented in a different way, or have an entirely different learning activity associated with it. This kind of reinforcement, I think, assists both in attention and retention.

Impact of Constant Information Availability and Asynchronicity on Memory

Memory is the first building block of learning. We talked earlier of the advantages of constructing knowledge and establishing meaning by associating new information with existing concepts stored in long-term memory. It is important to bear in mind that short-term memory can be affected by time, and as Levine (2002) points out, a new piece of information can erase a previously known fact, if it succeeds it too quickly. In fact, Levine is concerned that in the act of moving from one class immediately to another on campus, some information from the previous class might be blotted out. This points to an argument in favor of the online class, in which each participant can become absorbed and work hopefully without interruptions, and have sufficient time for the information to be fully comprehended. If this is so, it is more likely to stay in the mind for much longer. Furthermore, whereas the campus class meetings are at discrete intervals throughout the weeks, necessitating starting each new class by reviewing what had been covered in the previous class, the steady flow of information through online discussion, I think, assists learners in terms of holding their attention and helping them to retain this information.

The Significance of Active Learning on Knowledge Acquisition

For a thorough acquisition of knowledge, it is vital to have discussion about topics learned, which can be conducted effectively online, whether the class is a hybrid or is conducted entirely in cyberspace. Frequent feedback is helpful in letting students know how they are doing and in maintaining their motivation. The feedback must be encouraging so that it stresses the positive of the student's achievement before mentioning suggestions for improvement, as this reinforcement further increases motivation. Positive feedback is especially important online, where tone of voice and facial expression are absent, so that critical words can come across sounding more harsh than intended (see Part II). In this way, the online teacher is concerned with personalizing education and thus is responsive to each individual student.

Knowledge, Boettcher (1999) states, has the most chance of flourishing in an environment that is rich, supportive, encouraging, and enthusiastic. Students can pool their knowledge and learn new concepts, and feel safe admitting if they are confused. Admission of confusion is often a ripe launching point, if a new explanation is given, for the student to hopefully experience the wonderful feeling of pure insight and clarity, as the new concept makes sense and becomes meaningful.

The Importance of Awareness of Student Needs and Differing Abilities

It is only through online discussion that the instructor can come to know the students, and know how they think. Online discussion might shed light on difficulties faced by a student for whom English is a second language, or even on students with learning disabilities. Dyslexia, for example, could make the online class a perplexing place, and problems with written expression might inhibit the student from fully participating. Not knowing this about the student might lead the instructor to erroneously conclude that the student is not paying attention or is being lax about conforming to the minimum participation requirement. Becoming acquainted with one's students through online discussion might also inform the instructor that students are from different disciplinary backgrounds or that they have varying skills and interests.

It is in your students' interests, as much as is feasible, to be attentive to their particular needs. If you decide to adapt your class to match the array of cognitive styles among your students, you could do so either by enhancing your instructional materials or by varying your teaching style, or both (Liu and Ginther, 1999). Enhancing your materials might simply mean, for example, providing more diagrams alongside the written lectures, if you are aware that you have some students who are visual learners. Or, if you know about other courses that students are taking or their career goals, then perhaps you can provide examples of reinforcement within the context of the material you are teaching that are specific to their other interests and long-term goals.

As for varying your teaching style, it is probably a good idea in any case, even before knowing the strengths and weaknesses of your students, to aim to provide a mix of cooperative and individual learning, both of which can be done effectively online. Individual learning could include research papers or essays, whereas cooperative learning could embrace general discussion as well as group work of varying kinds.

Factors that Work against Knowledge Acquisition and Feeling of Community

Many factors could either enhance knowledge acquisition through online discussion or act as a deterrent. It is crucial to personalize the teaching approach, give frequent and encouraging feedback, and establish a good sense of camaraderie in the online class (see Chapter 2). Some conditions, however, can work against the potential for the acquisition of knowledge and a feeling of community. This can also be true for the campus class. On campus, for example, we know that the potential to process information can be severely reduced if more than one person speaks at a time, or if a session lasts beyond a student's attention span.

What are the deterrents to knowledge acquired online? One is the feeling of being overwhelmed, brought on by a large class, lengthy lectures or online responses, or numerous responsibilities outside the class. This might lead to the situation in which some students might not read everything that is contributed to the discussion, as it might seem an excessive amount. Perhaps one can argue that they are being selective, but they might be leaving out the most pertinent points.

A second deterrent involves technical difficulties, without timely and helpful technical support. Students benefit if, at the start of the online class, they take an orientation to learn how to navigate around the class, submit assignments, download from the Web, and so on. During the class, however, the student who experiences technical difficulties can feel panic or frustration. Some technical difficulties might affect the whole class, such as the server going down or a frequent generation of error messages. In this case, the instructor can reassure the class by changing due dates of submissions and empathizing with the expressed frustrations. If an individual student experiences frustrations of being unable to access the class or post responses, then the student should inform the instructor. If the excuse is legitimate and not a cyberversion of "the dog ate my homework," then some latitude should be given.

The Impact of Nonlinear Learning

No study of online learning theory is complete without considering the impact of nonlinear learning. In the campus class, students are used to learning chronologically in a linear progression through time. In contrast, the online class might have the potential for nonlinear learning, because it is an asynchronous environment and because of the layout of the discussion threads. There is a very real consequence of the way the discussion responses are displayed, and this varies with the different software programs. If the responses are laid out in a chronological fashion, I feel this would be more likely to lead to linear thought, as the discussion progresses along a linear time line. But many software programs have a threaded discussion, which means that messages are attached to the comments to which they are responding. This leads to a pattern in which responses are distributed thematically, not chronologically. Time, the great organizer, is now out of the equation, and we all have the possibility of dipping in and out of topics. This might be confusing to some, but liberating for others.

Online teaching might also lead to nonlinearity if hypertext is used. Hypertext fiction, for example, breaks free of the two-dimensional constraints of the printed page, and can lead off, by clicking on links, in many possible directions within a three-dimensional universe through a veritable cyberspatial labyrinth. The same applies to clicking on Web sites, whose links often lead to more Web sites, and then yet more. I think the question arises as to just how much clicking should we invite our students to do, before they become too disorientated, too dizzy, too remote from the place that is their online class?

The most interesting challenge about the existence of nonlinear learning in the online class is whether this is reflective of how our minds work and how our memory functions. Do we actually make mental leaps and start new threads within our thought processes when jolted by associations? Or, in our thinking, do we tunnel deeper and deeper along the same channel? Furthermore, just because technology makes nonlinear learning feasible, is it always desirable? Could it result in students each working independently, immersed in their own thought paths, and tackling questions and becoming excited by concepts at different rates and in different places from each other? If so, how can an instructor hold a cohesive class and encourage meaningful communication between and among all members of the class? Also, does it not depend on the subject matter being taught, because are there not some disciplines in which knowledge and understanding has to be accumulated sequentially? Could a student, for example, understand gravitational theory without first having a good grasp on how to calculate equations? Is the acquisition of knowledge all about building on what one has known before in a strictly linear fashion?

In turn, though, is this steady, linear acquisition of learning and knowledge overemphasizing the need for familiarity and comfort? I wonder whether it might be true to say that one needs some discomfort, some agitation, some tension to be challenged, to be creative, to find new thought pathways. I am a great admirer of Edward de Bono, who talked about paradigms of knowledge. He believed in the importance of creative lateral, not linear, thinking; of leaping out of the deep, linear hole of one paradigm to start a new paradigm elsewhere; and of thinking about a problem in a fresh, innovative way.

My personal feeling is that it is important to have a blend between linear thinking and lateral leaps into a new area where a new strand of linear thought can begin. I believe that the online environment can provide scope for both linear and lateral thought, but this is an enormous task and a dual role for the online instructor. The online instructor should allow for freedom within learning to make concepts meaningful, realizing that this can often be brought about by nonlinear, associative means. The instructor also must be a great facilitator in pulling together disparate strands of conversations, expertly weaving the different threads of expressed thought to make a cohesive body of knowledge, which can move forward in a linear fashion until it naturally starts to branch out again. This, I believe, leads to meaningful learning, as well as richness and diversity of thought and discussion.

How can we make practical use of these learning theories as applied to the online environment? It is to practical applications that we will now turn in Part II.

PART II
PRACTICAL APPLICATIONS

This section offers practical applications of the various learning theories discussed in Part I to online teaching so as to achieve inspirational results. Topics covered in this section include:

- Course design
- Starting to teach the online class
- Aspects of online communication
- Innovative online teaching techniques

4

COURSE DESIGN

Simplicity and repose are the qualities
that measure the true value of any
work of art "Think simple" as my old
master used to say—meaning reduce
the whole of its parts into the simplest
terms, getting back to first principles.
—*Frank Lloyd Wright, 1932*

As we have seen in Part I, it is both possible and indeed essential to establish a feeling of place in an online class, despite the fact that it does not
occupy physical space. If a student feels lonely or remote from the learning process, chances are that the potential for meaningful and inspirational education will be reduced. This section will discuss ways in
which a robust online course can be designed so as to enhance a feeling of
a community of learners. The energy of the online course occurs on the
discussion boards; and a thorough look at varying aspects of online communication will be given in Chapter 6. Let us first look at optimal ways
in which to construct the basics of an online course shell, before the students arrive, as the layout will have a big impact on the involvement of the
students and on the potential for discussion and deep learning to occur.

Customizing the Class

Biographical Statement and Syllabus

Before your class begins, you should fill out some biographical and contact information about yourself. It is also advisable to post your syllabus
online. Even if your class is a hybrid, it is beneficial for you to have your
syllabus reside online, so that no student can claim to have lost it. Your syl-

labus should contain information on your course description, course goals and objectives, readings, learning activities, grading policy, schedule, and expectations. It is important that you specify how frequently students are expected to log on to your class, and *participate* in discussions and activities. It is not enough to only stipulate how often students should log on, because they have no presence unless they participate. Also inform students that they should spread their time in your online class throughout the week, rather than, for example, only logging on four times each Friday.

One online instructor tells her students, whether online or on campus, a story entitled, "The Three Bricklayers," as a device whereby to inform them of her expectation of them. The story goes as follows:

> Once there were three bricklayers.
> Each one of them was asked what they were doing.
>
> The first man answered gruffly,
> "I'm laying bricks."
> The second man replied,
> "I'm putting up a wall."
> But the third man said enthusiastically and with pride,
> "I'm building a cathedral."
>
> —*Author Unknown*

This story, found online at www.wow4u.com/3bricks/, she believes helps students to identify the importance of attitude and how having a good attitude can lead to a more successful outcome. It helps students to see the importance of keeping an eye on the bigger picture so that rather than just doing the minimum and regarding it as an effort and a task, they can focus their energy and become more motivated. This is the difference between students simply logging on and those actively seeking to broaden their education.

Posting an Introductory Lecture

Having completed the syllabus, you should also post a first introductory lecture. Some instructors like to create all their lectures before the class begins, and make the later lectures unavailable to students until the appropriate time in the semester. Others like to create lectures as they proceed through the course. Either way works well, but what I recommend is not to have all the lectures of the entire course available to the student at the start of the semester, as online classes should not be self-paced. If they were self-paced, it could rapidly become hectic, and also there would be less scope for interaction. Instead, the lecture material should unfold throughout the semester, so as to best replicate what occurs in the campus class and to steadily and meaningfully progress through the course material.

Posting a First Discussion Forum

It is extremely beneficial to create a first discussion forum, which I like to call "The Virtual Lounge," specifically for all class participants to post personal introductions and to start to become acquainted. This reduces the chance of students feeling like they are sending out responses to the great unknown. Another advantage of this informal discussion forum is that it gives new online students some practice and experience with online discussions before needing to respond to specific, formal course content. I recommend that students should be invited to return to "The Virtual Lounge" throughout the semester, so as to maintain a feeling of camaraderie. Indeed, I have found that students use this area exactly like a lounge. Online discussions are studied in more depth in Chapter 6.

Posting an Announcement

You should also post an announcement, the area for which is positioned on the first screen that students will read when they log in to your class. The announcement area is a sort of in-between place, a virtual spot whose primary function is to point the way to other places; in fact, I like to think of it as equivalent to C.S. Lewis's "Wood Between the Worlds" in his marvelous story, *The Magician's Nephew.* As in Lewis's tale, it should be a friendly and welcoming place, as many new students might be feeling apprehensive in the same way that they had felt on their first day of school. As well as greeting your students, your announcement could inform them as to how to navigate around your online class, so that they can visit all its virtual rooms, such as your biographical statement, the syllabus, the lecture area, and the discussion forums (see Figure 1: Example of an Online Announcement).

Signposts

> You must walk. It is a long journey, through a country that is sometimes pleasant and sometimes dark and terrible. . . . "The road to the City of Emeralds is paved with yellow brick," said the Witch, "so you cannot miss it." (Excerpt from *The Wonderful Wizard of Oz*, by L. Frank Baum)

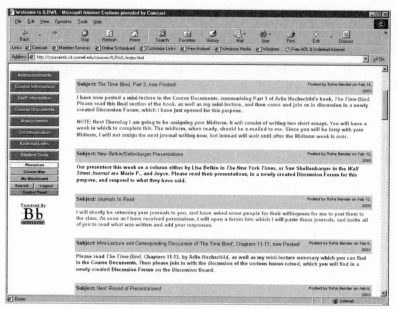

Figure 1   Example of an Online Announcement

Since the announcement area therefore can serve as a directional board, let us look more specifically at the question of creating clear signposts within your online class. This is of the utmost importance, as the goal is to make the technology as transparent and seamless as possible. In this way, students do not expend all their energy on wondering where to click to achieve a desired end, but can focus on the course content itself. After all, online classes are just an alternative method of delivery and communication of information, and to me the fascination does not lie in the technology that takes us there, but in the course material itself. It seems to me to be directly analogous to driving a car; we learn to operate it, but for most of us, the emphasis is not on how the car works, but on the fact that it takes us to our destination.

Imagine you have arrived at a new college campus for an important function such as an interview or because you have been invited as a guest lecturer. Consequently you need to find your way, possibly with some urgency, to the right department. Now, maybe you will ask some people who you see strolling around the campus to direct you to the correct building, or maybe you will search for signposts. In either case, you might feel somewhat stressed, and would be grateful for as many clear directions as possible.

Now translate this into the cyberspatial campus. Imagine how students feel as they not only find their way to your course, but also try to navigate around the various virtual rooms you have established within your class. They also experience a feeling of urgency and possibly a little anxiety, just as you might when visiting an unfamiliar campus, as they want to quickly see what your class entails and what they need to do. In fact, the need for clear directions and signposts might be magnified in the cyberspatial campus, because in this virtual world, form does not reflect function, as is generally the case in the real world.

So how best do you provide signposts in your online class? First, I advise that if you have chosen fancy names for any of the virtual rooms in your class, make sure you have explained your terms so that no students will feel lost or confused. It might also be helpful to provide information as to how to return home to the announcement area.

I recommend using the announcement area not only at the start of the semester to help students navigate around your online class, but also throughout the duration of the course to give information. For example, it can be used for keeping students informed about due dates, pertinent course-related news on the media, relevant museum exhibits, and so on. Try to make each new announcement a different color from the last so that they are eye-catching and thus more apt to be read. If yours is a software program in which each new announcement replaces the previous one, then it is important to keep each announcement up long enough to ensure that students, working asynchronously, will all have a chance to see it.

The question then arises as to how often must you repeat information. A colleague of mine emphasized the importance of redundancy in an online course, as she believed in posting the same information in many areas of the course. Another school of thought, however, is to resist redundancy on the grounds that it might insult the intelligence of students and therefore lead them to skip over these kinds of postings; and once a skipper, maybe always a skipper, tripping and skipping over other, more salient information. In fact, you want the students to read everything, every word you post, and certainly all the responses of their classmates.

In certain areas I do think repetition might be a good and necessary idea. With an assignment, for example, you might want to give the directions, such as length, due date, and method of submission, both in the assignment itself and in the announcement area. You might also want to repeat information in the announcement area that is contained in your syllabus, or remind students to revisit the syllabus (which some students might otherwise look at only once at the start of the semester). If you receive an e-mail from a student asking where to go in the course for a particular function, or when to expect certain events such as midterms or finals, you might want to answer this as a general announcement in class, because chances are that if this student lost her or his sense of direction, others might well have felt the same way.

Also, while on the topic of signposting, I think it enormously important to carefully streamline information of particular types and not allow confusing overflows. Again, this helps students to know where to find or post different types of information. You need to clearly construct your discussion board so that students understand at a glance the topic of each discussion. An online class that has a discussion board containing a dull list of topics, labeled "Discussion 1," "Discussion 2," and so on, might confuse students and certainly will not spark their interest in the same way as a representative or catchy title to the discussion topic would do.

Even with careful directions, though, errors might occasionally occur. I have occasionally had a student post a response in the wrong forum. In terms of the interruption to the flow of conversation, I was immediately reminded of being once deeply immersed in a complicated recipe in a cook book for which I had no great fondness, and being up to my elbows in flour, only to be told to now turn to page 152. In cases of posting to the wrong forum, it might be best for you to paste it in to the correct forum and delete it from its original position before confusion mounts. It is also a good idea to send an e-mail to the author of that response, saying what you have done and why it was necessary.

Arrangement of Lecture Material

What is the optimal way of dividing up your lecture material so that it is logical, crisp and clear in format, and most readily comprehended by students? I would like to suggest that the course objectives should seem feasible and relevant, and that the course is well sequenced to allow logical progression from easier to more difficult concepts and tasks. If a jump is made too rapidly to difficult tasks or concepts, students might feel alienated, lack self-confidence, and might perhaps drop the course. As the students progress along the spectrum from simpler to harder tasks, you as the instructor might need to reinforce concepts that serve as building blocks to knowledge. Reinforcement does not necessarily mean repetition, but could be done through a different activity, as in this way you might reach different types of learners (Vella, 1997).

I suggest one of the following four alternatives to divide up your lecture material.

- *Thematic divisions:* You organize your material according to theme or topic. For example, in my "Ethics and the Family" course, I have thematic divisions such as the effect on family when one member commits a crime, when there is divorce, and so on. This format might work well for many courses in the humanities, social sciences, education, and health-related fields.

- *Chronological divisions:* If you are teaching a literature course, you could, for example, divide your lectures by literature published in different time periods. This type of structure work well for a course in any discipline that has as its basis a historical emphasis.

- *Divided by different books studied:* An alternative structure for a literature course is to divide according to the books to be read and analyzed. For example, in a course on D.H. Lawrence, you could open separate lecture documents for *Sons and Lovers, The Rainbow, Women in Love,* and *Lady Chatterley's Lover.*

- *Divided by chapters in a book:* This format might be effective for any course that follows the basic structure of a textbook. If the textbook has a large number of chapters, it might be advantageous, if possible, to "bundle" a few chapters together in each lecture.

The Online Lecture Format

I recommend that the instructor post short, succinct, snappy lectures, more appropriately called "mini-lectures". By doing this, I am keeping Frank Lloyd Wright's words about the advantage of simplicity clearly in mind. If the lecture is too long (taking up more than a few screens), students might feel they could more easily be reading a book on a comfortable sofa, rather than sitting at a computer terminal. Excessively long lectures also lessen the opportunities for interactivity. If you feel your lecture is becoming too lengthy, divide it up into two or more mini-lectures of a more digestible size.

I also recommend that you create a corresponding dicussion forum to accompany each mini-lecture, as this offers not only the opportunity for students to react to your mini-lecture, but also provides you with an opportunity to continue to give students information that might otherwise have been part of your lecture, but is now offered as a series of responses within the discussion. By this means, your information is unfolding in segments within an interactive framework.

Some professors are initially concerned about limiting the length of their lectures as they think the students might lose out on valuable information. I would say that this method does not dilute the information you are providing your students; it is instead repackaging it and parceling some out within discussion, to suit the online environment and promote interactivity (see Figure 2: Example of an Online Mini-Lecture).

Having now taken into explicit consideration the pertinent issues relating to course design, you are now ready to start teaching. And it is to the factors surrounding starting to teach an online course that is the focus of the next chapter.

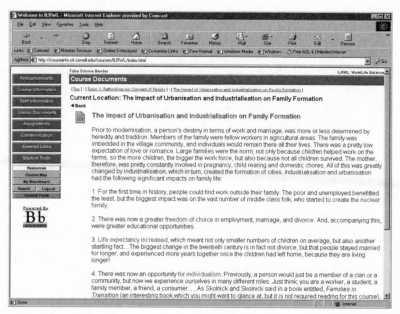

Figure 2   Example of an Online Mini-Lecture

5

STARTING TO TEACH THE ONLINE CLASS

Teachers open the door, you enter
by yourself.
            —*Chinese Proverb*

Ideally your institution will offer some sort of online orientation for new students before their course begins. They should be given their user ID and password in advance, and should be told the URL of your online course. The orientation should include a hands-on experience of the online environment, so as to become familiar with it, or, if you are teaching a hybrid class, it would be advantageous if your institution has prepared a handout explaining the basics of navigating through your online course, and you could spend some time in your campus class going through this. It has been found that students who are given a basic orientation to the online environment do better than those who do not, as they can start to focus more quickly on the course content rather than on basic operations.

So, the students should be ready for their online class, but what about you? Some new online instructors report feeling quite anxious before they start to teach; I heard one instructor say it felt like "navigating in the dark," and another say that she felt as though she "did not know where the chalk was." It is to varying forms of instructor anxiety, and methods to alleviate it, that we now turn our attention.

Anxiety

Campus teaching and online teaching involve different sets of worries. On campus there is the worry, especially before the first class, as to how to effectively grab each student's interest and sustain that over the allotted time slot; the worry about blanking out and looking stupid; the worry about how long it will take to remember every student's name; the worry about the suitability of the room and whether the arrangement of furniture is flexible; the worry that any and all equipment which might be needed for your class to run smoothly is present and in working order; maybe the worry about whether the new shoes you have bought will pinch your toes; the worry about the possibility of delays in the journey to class. Online you can be comforted about not having to worry about new shoes, delayed journeys, memorizing names, seating arrangements, or keeping everyone interested for a rigid time period, but it does not mean a total freedom from worries. Instead there is the worry about whether the technology will cooperate; the worry of making what might feel like an indelible error; the worry that your students might understand computers better than you do; the consequent worry that you might lose command of the class; and the worry about being insufficiently prepared. We have talked about preparing your course shell, and since you will have put a lot of thought and deliberation into your course design, it will have the potential of being a stimulating and fulfilling class.

Remember, anxiety is common when faced with any new enterprise, and a little nervousness about teaching is normal, is likely to be felt by others, and can actually be tapped to enhance good teaching, as long as it does not become overwhelming (Teaching and Educational Development Institute [TEDI], 2002). Some instructors let the students know that this is their first time teaching online, and they might even tell them they are a little anxious. This immediately helps, I believe, as the instructor is not so worried about trying to impress, and probably, as a result of letting students know, is likely to do a better job. Also, spending a few days in your "Virtual Lounge" before embarking on course content can make the students seem *human* as you become acquainted, rather than part of a long list of names on a screen. When teaching, as soon as I read responses from my students and enter into conversations with them, my nervousness subsides. By then we are involved together in the academic pursuit of the subject matter, and the excitement of the voyage has begun.

Means of Engagement

Ideally we should strive to involve our students to such an extent in the joy of learning that they become deeply immersed (Vella, 1997). We can tell this occurs online when their comments are frequent and involved, as well as being deep, thoughtful, insightful, and excited. This is the pitch that we as teachers enjoy.

However, even if students participate in an orientation, they still may not always enter your online class promptly. I had always expected that as soon as the virtual classroom door swung open at the start of the semester, my students would come pouring through, but this has not always been the case for all students, as there have been delays over acquiring passwords, technical difficulties, and any manner of cyberspatial excuses. Even though the online environment is an asynchronous one, we want to avoid having stragglers who pull the discussion in a backward direction by their late participation; and ideally we want everyone in the class to be involved in the same discussion at approximately the same time.

The following sections provide suggestions as to how to engage students so that the online class is off to a sizzling start.

The Benefits of Contacting Each Student Individually at the Start of the Semester

It might be productive to assess individual student needs before the class begins, either by phone or in person (Vella, 1997). Generally in classes taught completely online, I have found that students have been gratified to receive a call, and it provides the additional benefit of making the teacher seem more of a real person to them. Students in hybrid classes might too be helped by this individual contact, as it can lead to better understanding as to *why* they should log on to the Web component of their class, and what they will *gain* in the process.

Designing an Informal First Discussion Topic

I think it is in both your and your students' interests to design a first discussion topic that is so enticing, so intriguing, and so marvelous that they really do not want to miss out on it. In other words, by providing a meaningful challenge from the start, you are giving students an opportunity for engagement.

We have talked about constructing a "Virtual Lounge", but what should be the initial topic of conversation? In what ways can you thaw the online "ice crystals" before the course content begins? The expression, "Start as you mean to go on," generally echoes through my mind at the start of any class, as time and time again, I see that a class which starts with a great deal of enthusiasm and energy generally maintains that dynamism, whereas a class with a few straggling and occasional remarks is often harder to spark.

Asking Students to Discuss Relevant Experiences in Their Personal Introductions

You might want to not only ask students to introduce themselves, but also to ask a few questions that are relevant to the context of your course and define its parameters. For example, if you are teaching a writing class, you might ask what students have already written; or in a literature course, you ask what else they have read in this particular genre. You might choose to ask students to "free associate," and write anything that comes to mind as stimulated by a word or words in your course name (TEDI, 2002).

Completing a Sentence

Another idea is to start a sentence and ask students to complete it. For example, write, "I was riding the subway today, when I . . ." Students generally love to see what others have written and enjoy interacting with each other immediately. Your sentence prompt could be about anything, but it might be helpful to tailor it, even subtly, to the subject matter of your course.

Students Interview and Introduce Each Other

Some instructors ask students to confess a secret that they have cherished, and the conversation can actually become quite amusing. Others ask students to interview each other, especially with questions related to the course topic, and then present an introduction about the interviewee.

Providing a Hook

One instructor, as an icebreaker, asked students to tell about the "weirdest gift" they had ever received. She later used this as an analogy to some aspect of their course content, which was on special education services. Other instructors, myself included, like to tell just a snippet of a personal anecdote, as this can provide a hook onto which students can tell related stories. Telling the latest adventures of the new and naughty tricks of my dog, Homer, for example, generally inspires others to relate a bit about their pets, too.

Visualization Techniques

Some instructors like to use visualization techniques, such as asking students to imagine they are sitting together in a comfortable classroom, preferably in a circle, which eradicates the feeling of hierarchy. Others paint a cozier picture, by telling students that this class will be run like a symposium, the true meaning of which is getting together and drinking with friends, while discussing topics of mutual interest. Hull (2002), conjured up to her online students at New York University, the image of sitting with friends on the porch of an old country house during a delightful summer evening, sipping tea. I think these methods help prod the imagination into making up for any deficits in sensory stimuli of the online class.

Playing a Game

Another idea that I have seen used to good effect is to immediately involve students in playing a game. One such example is the game of the sinking ship, in which there is only one lifeboat left, with a capacity of twelve passengers, yet there are twenty passengers left on the ship. The instructor gives detailed descriptions of nineteen passengers, by age, occupation, family status, income level, state of health, and so on, and with an added flourish, says the twentieth passenger is you! The challenge is to determine who should be allowed on the lifeboat. As you can imagine, a game of this nature immediately captures the imagination and appeals to the sense of excitement and adventure. The game could be used as an example of a concept taught later in the class, such as, by analogy, a corporate decision such as downsizing.

Asking Students What They Hope to Learn from the Course

Using the story, "The Three Bricklayers," as a way to exemplify differ-ent attitudes to learning, the instructor asks her students to name their own learning objectives, which is a great way of encouraging students to take responsibility. Although she does not mention it, it seems that from here the instructor and students could develop a learning con-tract, and if students want to learn more about areas that have not been included in the syllabus, then she could offer them individual research projects.

Asking Students to Write Short Descriptive Stories about Themselves

Jack A. Cummings, professor of Counseling and Educational Psychol-ogy at Indiana University, speaks of how he asked students to choose eight nouns which best describe themselves, and requested that each stu-dent write a short paragraph to elaborate upon these nouns (Cummings, 1998). His own paragraph descriptions were so lovely that if I had been a student in his class, I would have warmed up to him immediately. For example, one noun he used to describe himself was *cyclist,* and this is what he said:

> I have enjoyed riding bicycles since my parents bought a bike that was way too big for me when I was about five. I had to stand on an over-turned bucket to even get on it. My feet only reached the pedals for about half a revolution. Now, riding through the hills of southern Indiana keeps me sane. My goal is to ride 3 to 5 times a week. On a good week, I sometimes get in three rides. The piles of paper in my office keep me chained to the desk.

Cummings recognized, in posting this information, that he was much more wordy than he would have been if he was meeting his stu-dents on campus, but online he did not have a time restraint, so he did not feel the need to summarize quite so much. He recognized a few other differences as well, between online and face-to-face discussion. For example, just as he could write his introduction in a leisurely fash-ion, so could everyone else, which was different, he said, from the cam-pus setting in which, as student contributions are sequential, the ones asked last to contribute their introduction often have to rush before the end of the class session. Online, everyone can respond at virtually the same time, without taking up time from each other. Also, when students are asked to introduce themselves in a face-to-face classroom situation, many times they are so busy rehearsing what they are going to say, or so nervous about when it will be their turn, that they do not listen carefully to their classmates. Not so online!

Furthermore, Cummings points out, there is a permanent record of everyone's response, so if anyone wants to refresh their memory, they can simply click back to reread a student's comment. As a result of these fuller and more explicit introductions from the students, Cummings believes he became acquainted with each of the students much more quickly than in the campus class, in which it might take until midsemester to know just the more vocal students. I might add that it is also advantageous to the students as they too become familiar with each other quickly, and it eases their comfort level in participating in discussions of class content. Cummings illustrates a few student paragraph descriptions, my favorite of which is entitled "Ankle Twister":

> Ankle twister—Ever since I was a child, I have been falling on concrete, tripping on carpet, falling off my bike, and slipping on the ice. I am a very clumsy person by nature and I've sprained my ankle every year of my life. Attractive? . . . Many see this quality as simply irresistible.

I have tried a similar technique of asking students to write short stories about themselves in my online classes, often to good effect. For example, in one online class on international children's literature, I asked students to complete the following sentence: "When I was young, I traveled to [you fill in the location] and the most outstanding part of my visit was when I . . ." I then went ahead and composed my story first, as a way to illustrate to students the scope and possibilities of this exercise. I wrote:

> When I was young, I traveled to Lyons, France, to visit my French pen-pal, and the most outstanding part of my visit was when I was foolish enough to show off the few words of French that I knew to my pen-pal's mother, even though the words themselves were untrue. I brashly said, *"Je fais le regime!"* (I am on a diet) at which this

remarkable French woman, robust and with a kitchen full of tempting ingredients, declared, "*Moi aussi!*" and that started my two weeks of terrific hunger. We would pass the boulanger, the windows full of baguettes and croissants, brioches and tempting and beautiful pastries, and my mouth would water. We would walk in the square, past the street market, and I'd have to be dragged from the counters with slabs of pâté, delicately thin sliced meats, frilly vegetables, and chocolate truffles. I would stare up at the grand, ornate stone buildings, thinking only of how the two *tranches de jambon* (slices of ham), which made up my entire dinner, made me feel hungrier still. But one fine day we had a visit into the country, to see my pen-pal's grandmother, and she put before me a steaming bowl full of soft, buttery, creamy pastina, and I will always remember how truly satisfying that tasted.

I received some wonderful student stories in return. One student from Texas visited Switzerland, and having never seen snow before, built her sister into a snowman. Another student traveled alone to the Philippines and shared this story:

> It was the beginning of hurricane season high up in the mountains and all I remember of the last half of our stay was sitting on the toilet in the bathroom wondering if porcelain could conduct electricity. My mother yelled at me for spending over $10.00 on a long distance phone call just to ask her that.

In an online writing class, I started by asking students to complete the sentence, "Yesterday morning I received a letter from my close friend Julie, in Australia, and she said that whenever she thinks of me she thinks . . ." I asked them to include within that letter at least *three statements* which best describe themselves. I again went first with my letter, and received some exceptionally witty responses back from students, which helped us to get to know each other and to positively look forward to reading future responses. Following are excerpts from the students' writings.

> In a conversation with friends, Julie said she spoke of me proudly and my ability to remain a vegan, even though I live with a chocolate lover and am tempted daily by one and all. She herself tries to give up meat, but those darn Australian steakhouses are so tantalizing!

I received a letter from my friend Julie in Australia today and she said when she thinks of me she thinks about how heartily I laugh and how contagious my laugh is. She says she can still hear my outbursts of laughter through the living room walls when she lived next door to me

Quite a temper but a great judge of character, usually. I remember once we argued about the origins of cynicism all night. She proceeded to ramble something about how I was trying to be a cynic and even though I had an amazing "cynically-laced facade" she could see right through me. Apparently unbeknownst to myself I was an "idealist" in both thought and action. She was right. Julie was a trip.

You know she was always saying the semi-right thing at the more than wrong time . . .

hmmm . . .

kind of glad she went back [to Australia].

Spending time at the start of the course to become familiar with the students, in any of the various ways mentioned, is crucial (1) to establishing an atmosphere of trust, enjoyment and excitement, (2) to engaging them in future work throughout the semester, and (3) in being able to accurately assess their learning outcomes by the completion of the course.

Establishing the Right Tone

The TEDI (2002) article mentions the importance, if teaching on campus, of maintaining a confident demeanor as you stand before your students, and that you have a clear, energetic tone of voice, that you smile, maintain eye contact, and speak with enthusiasm. This will establish you in the student's minds as not only being an expert in your subject, but also being a good communicator of that information, and thus a good teacher.

With an enjoyment of and competence in writing, this same sort of enthusiasm can be conveyed online, not only through your choice of words, but also through your responsiveness to your students. Above all, it is important to convey to the students that your online class is a safe place in which all responses are welcomed and encouraged. Obviously feelings of safety and security (which help to promote collaborative learning) do not come all at once, and cannot be there just because you tell the students it is a safe place. Instead you, as the instructor, need to instill it. You can do this by setting a warm, enthusiastic tone, and by replying to students, so that they are encouraged to check back to see if anyone responded to their comment. (For further discussion on safety in the online class, see in Chapter 6, "How We Show We Are Listening and Caring Online.")

When students feel recognized and acknowledged by the instructor, which is usually their first priority, they can then start becoming familiar with each other, and it is in this way that trust gradually starts to build up. In addition, a warm, conversational tone can be combined effectively with a rigorous academic approach, in which there is challenge and discourse, leading to an extensive exploration of the subject matter. Remember that you want to be a good role model for your students at all times, and you want them to consider you approachable.

Whichever icebreaker activity you choose to do at the start of the semester, I recommend that you post the first response, as this not only provides the students with guidelines and a good model, but also helps to establish the tone that you would like your class to take. It is particularly important from the start of the semester to be encouraging and supportive. The tone of your conversation is important, as it can serve either to distance you from your students or bring you into a closer circle. I recommend that you adopt a conversational style, as this assists in overcoming feelings of coldness or remoteness that working online might otherwise bring. You want as much as possible to make the online class feel like an exciting forum, in which real people are speaking to each other about mutually fascinating ideas.

Students might never before have experienced asynchronous discussions within an academic framework, so you need to do what you can to help make them not only feel welcomed but also at their peak to do their best work. I particularly recommend that you log on frequently during the early days of the class, to acknowledge students by name when commenting on their responses, so that they know you have noticed them and they feel included in the group. It is wise, when commenting on students' initial responses, to ask another question so that the conversation continues.

It is frequently amazing to me how students unknowingly mimic the tone of the instructor. If you, as instructor, answer briefly and curtly, students will answer in kind. If you post long responses, chances are that the students' responses will be long. Often, instructors who post infrequently and have brief responses that do not address every student's comment, do not encourage discussion.

An additional topic is how instructors prefer to be addressed by their students. Some instructors, in an effort to make for maximum conviviality and the decrease of hierarchy, ask students to call them by their first names, whereas others might prefer more formality. One observation I have made is that students generally treat faculty more informally in the online setting, but if this is not your preference, certainly let students know. It is also beneficial to ask students what they would like to be called. They may want to be called by their name posted on the screen, or they may have a nickname or other preference. I should mention, as an aside, that I came across one instructor who liked to call all his students by their last name, Mr. Smith, Ms. Jones, and so on. Certainly he gave to his class a most delightfully old-fashioned Oxford or Cambridge atmosphere, and one could almost imagine old dons gliding along wood paneled corridors.

Having established ways in which to successfully engage students in the introductory stages of the online course, the concern now shifts to sustaining active participation on the part of all students, throughout the duration of the semester. The Discussion Forums are the life blood and center of energy of the online class, and it is to methods of stimulating online discussion which we will now turn in Chapter 6.

6

ASPECTS OF ONLINE COMMUNICATION

Let me not to the marriage of true
minds
Admit impediment.
　　　　—Shakespeare, Sonnet 116

How to Facilitate and Stimulate Online Discussion

We have talked about how students benefit from an online orientation to gain the technical information needed to navigate through their online class, and we have talked about including an icebreaker activity in the "Virtual Lounge" of your online class, so as to help everyone become acquainted in the initial days of the semester. These, according to Gilly Salmon, are the first two steps in the learner's development, which she calls "Access and Motivation," and "Online Socialization," respectively (Salmon, 2000).

Having now gained familiarity with the technology, and having developed a general idea of the personality and interests of the instructor and classmates, the time is ripe for the learning of the course material to begin. This next step, which Salmon (2000) calls "Information Exchange," is the stage at which rigorous interactive discussion takes place, and it is to the techniques for promoting a good, in-depth discussion that this section will turn attention. My basic premise is that learning is best achieved through dialogue. Dialogue comes from the word *dia*, meaning "between," and *logos*, meaning "word" (Vella, 1997). In this way, we can think of teaching and learning as being comprised and communicated by the words that flow between teacher and student, as well as student and student.

I believe that online teaching and learning has the potential to produce a true meeting of minds, because, being as it is, devoid of information which is extraneous in most courses, about factors such as age, race, possibly gender, and even such stereotypical distractions as clothing, hairstyle, accents of speech, and so on, one can fully concentrate on the intellects, interests, and personalities of the participants. It is, in essence, a democratic system, in which ideas and information are free to swirl in all directions. How can we fully realize this potential and establish the setting for a completely satisfying and rich online discussion? The following ideas suggest how this might be encouraged.

Clearly Define Your Expectations for Discussion

Frequency of Participation

State at the beginning of the course how often you want your students to log on and *participate*. I emphasize that students should participate, because just logging on is not sufficient. Unless you "hear" from your students in their responses, there is little you can know about them. Also provide students with a clear idea as to how often they can expect you to be in class. Some instructors who operate better with structure, like to be definitive about when they will log on, saying, for example, that they will be there every Monday, Wednesday, and Friday from 11:00 to 1:00. Others, making fuller use of the flexibility of the online environment, prefer to say that they will be logging on at least four times per week. Stipulating the approximate frequency of logging on to class without specifying time slots allows you, if you have an inspirational thought at 3 A.M. to grab it while it is still fresh and exciting, and enter it into your class. Similarly, you are not disappointing students if a sudden meeting comes up at the same time you told students you would be online.

Making explicit the frequency of your participation in class helps students to anticipate when they will be hearing from you, and also will not give false impressions that just because the class is available 24 × 7, that you are, too. Try to be realistic about how frequently you can participate in your online class. One instructor told his class he would do so every day, and then, when on certain occasions he found this to be impossible, some students felt disappointed about not hearing from him.

Participation Counts Toward the Final Grade

You can make participation count significantly toward the final grade, but it should not only be a quantitative measure. After all, you cannot measure the success of a certain dish by the number of times the chef enters the kitchen. So the *quality* of response has to count as well. A student who logs on five times over two days only to say, "I agree with Miranda," for example, is obviously not contributing as much as another student who logs on only once during that time period, but contributes a thoughtful, substantive, insightful response. Generally I have found that as the semester progresses, the class gathers a momentum of its own as certain topics heat up, and at these times some students participate several times a day!

If participation in discussion counts significantly toward the final grade, then it would be fair to let students know how they are doing at specific intervals throughout the semester, rather than leaving this a mystery until the end. Timing, however, is crucial. You do not want to grade the discussion of a particular topic until you are sure it is completed, as otherwise it will stifle further responses. If you let students know that you will be grading discussion topics, it might be a helpful incentive to motivate them to discuss the topic in a timely manner, rather than entering a discussion too late.

Style of Online Responses

Let students know that online discussion should have the feeling of a seminar. In one of the first online classes I taught, I had a student with whom I had spoken on the phone at the beginning of the semester, and was immediately struck by how articulate, enthusiastic, and intelligent she sounded. Yet five days elapsed and there were no online responses from her. Surprised by this, I called her again. She explained her silence by saying that she thought she had to write something very formal in the online discussion, complete with an outline and footnotes. I told her the time for that sort of polish was in the written papers and exams.

The online discussion, I informed her, was just that—an opportunity for bouncing intelligent, informative ideas off each other in a spontaneous stream of consciousness. Of course the hope is that student responses will not be full of grammatical and spelling mistakes, but I think it advisable that they feel that they are "talking" rather than composing an essay. Once I clarified my expectations both with her and the rest of the students, the class positively exploded with responses from everyone.

Discuss Rules for Civility

Blankespoor (1996) tells his students at the start of the semester that the class is like a "family" for a semester, and just as in a family, everyone should be "positive, sensitive, considerate, polite and tolerant." I inform my students that I love to thrash around in a thorough discussion of a topic from multiple perspectives, as I believe this is the stuff of good, balanced considerations. I welcome everyone's response, even if it runs counter to the prevailing ideology, as long as all responses can be substantiated. Often the soundest learning is brought about through passionate argument, but this should be accompanied by mutual respect and toleration of differing viewpoints. Guidelines for this type of respectful debate are essential not only for the smooth functionality of the online class, but also because learning civil behavior is ultimately crucial for the student's survival in a pluralistic world, and for them to learn how to participate in rigorous challenges and exchange of ideas (Baldwin, 2000).

Once guidelines of civility are drawn up, it is important for faculty not to go into denial if rude or inappropriate behavior is occurring in the class, as this would imply that they are condoning this behavior. Furthermore, it would be a good idea for faculty to include a wide variety of teaching methods and learning activities, so that students with diverse skills and learning styles have a more equitable chance for full involvement. Instructors should learn student names (something which is easy to do online) and show an interest in each of them by responding frequently and thoughtfully to their comments.

There are various examples of student rudeness on campus, including lateness or leaving early, napping, reading a newspaper, speaking with each other rather than being attentive to the class, and possibly even threatening or actually physically attacking a professor over a grade (Schneider, 1998). Some students might even chat on their cell phones during classes. Although these circumstances can only occur in face-to-face situations, it does not mean that the online class is guaranteed to be free of expressions of incivility or lack of consideration. For example, a student who posts a very late response well after the class has moved on to a new topic is unfair and inconsiderate in expecting the collective class attention to be reverted to this previous topic. Online students also can be impolite or disrespectful in their remarks to each other or to the professor.

Perhaps students might behave in an uncivil manner because of the greater mix of diverse backgrounds, each with their own differing value system, or because the subject matter of the course seems esoteric (Baldwin, 2000). I believe that some students might feel unhappy in very large campus classes because of the remoteness from the professor and consequent feelings of anonymity. This certainly points to an advantage of adding a Web component to such a class, as the students could be split into smaller online groups and thus gain an increased means of communication and a better opportunity for becoming acquainted. This decrease in a sense of isolation through online discussion opportunities might reduce the likelihood of bad, attention-getting behavior from some disruptive students.

Should the instructor seek student opinions when making decisions that affect the class, or is it better for the instructor alone to make decisions? (Anderson and Adams, 1992). I advocate seeking student opinions, though of course I recognize that this might depend on the discipline of the course and the class size. As well as making explicit statements at the start of the semester about civility, involve students in drawing up a desired code of conduct, saying that everyone has a right to participate in its creation and that it is a living document which will evolve throughout the semester as situations change, as long as everyone is in agreement. I found that because students were directly and democratically involved in the creation of this code, and it was, therefore, a contract entered into together, they were more likely to keep to it. The only thing left to be decided upon, if you involve students in the creation of a code of conduct, is the system of enforcement. I found that students wanted to avoid "virtual finger-pointing" at each other when there was noncompliance, and preferred for me, as instructor, to take this role. Student opinion on this might vary, though, as some might want to take full responsibility not only for evolving the original contract but also for enforcement.

Employ the Socratic Method

Which is the better method in online teaching, lecturing to the students or employing the Socratic method? I would like to illustrate this debate by presenting a fictitious dialogue between two online professors. Although it is fictitious, it is the sort of dialogue I have heard, and maybe you have as well. Alternatively, maybe you have spoken some of these exact words yourself.

> SALLY: I'm setting up my online class and I'm definitely going to devote the first couple of days to personal introductions and shared anecdotes.
> BILL: I hate that "touchy-feely" sort of stuff. I want to let my students know that learning is serious, and we are getting right down to business. I suppose, throughout the semester, you encourage students to continue being "anecdotal."
> SALLY: Absolutely! I very much believe that students should relate their education to personal experiences, as that way it is more relevant and meaningful to them.
> BILL: I couldn't disagree more! What students want to pay all that money only to waste their time hearing trivial personal information from their classmates rather than instruction from their professor?

I think the subtext of this conversation is that no one can say with certainty which is the best approach to take. Most university instructors have not had teacher training, and what is more, they perform their teaching usually in the isolation of their own classroom or online course shell. When instructors talk with each other, it is more likely to be about the curriculum content than the method of communicating that content.

We teach in our own unique way. We have been conditioned, of course, by our own personal histories in general, and by profound teachers or mentors, by whom we were lucky enough to be taught, in particular. Both our upbringing and the influences on us as students will contribute toward our educational values and teaching techniques.

Furthermore, we are currently influenced not only by the institution in which we teach, but also by the students who occupy our classes.

The greatest unknown and the current influential element each semester, therefore, is the student body. But, online, how else can we know who these students are, unless we hear from them? How can we know that our lectures have been read and understood unless we read our students' reactions to them? True, some software programs have tracking devices whereby we can see what a student has supposedly read, but unless a student responds to questions from the lecture, how can we be certain that the student did not merely log on to the lecture and then take the dog for a walk? My feeling about the tracking device is that it is actually more informative about what students have not read than what they supposedly have read.

I agree with Sally's viewpoint from the dialogue; namely, that students learn in a meaningful way when they are encouraged to actively and deliberately explore the links between education, prior knowledge, and personal experience, and respond accordingly. And I agree with Charles Kerns in his view that it is beneficial for students to exert control over their learning and have the possibility of reflection, assessment, and co-construction of knowledge (quoted by Young, 2002).

Therefore, I do not advocate a purely lecture mode of instruction, in which the implicit assumption is that students, like newborn babies, are empty vessels in need of filling with knowledge. Instead, I think more can be gained online within a highly interactive environment.

Establish a Circle of Learning

It is quite amazing how relatively quickly students begin to recognize each other's voice, as everyone's unique personality radiates through their response. For this to happen, however, students must be informed at the beginning of the semester that they should actively engage in online discussion. Rather than there being a hierarchical structure to discussions, encourage interactivity between students as well as from students to you. Students appreciate hearing from you frequently within the discussion forum, to know you are completely involved in the collaborative online conversations. Even though you, the instructor, are in the same circle of learning as the students, you still have the prerogative to guide the discussion, introduce new concepts, and steer things along, much as parents do within the family circle (Dewey, 1938).

Encourage Students to be Active Learners

Encouragement of active participation from the students, as they contribute to the evolving dialogue, stimulates student learning. As Dewey (1938) states: "I assume that amid all uncertainties there is one permanent frame of reference; namely the organic connection between education and personal experience." Similarly, Fisher (2001) says, "Education cannot take place without some degree of self-disclosure" (p. 138). If information is seen as being meaningful and relevant, thus stimulating students to draw on their knowledge and experience, then true learning is taking place.

However, it is important to draw the right balance between a class that is too much of an "ivory tower," and one that slips into an excessive amount of personal, anecdotal discussions. The online environment can be alluring for some students, and with the protection of relative anonymity behind their computer screen, they can dip into more tales of intimacy than is common in the campus class (see "How We Show We Are Listening and Caring Online" later in the chapter). Brookfield and Preskill (1999) believe that a personal narrative is acceptable, as long as it is accompanied by critical thinking, in which the student can perhaps understand his or her experience from a new perspective. In some skills-based classes, students might already be working in the field, and it could be beneficial to ask them to relate their experiences, and also to make comparisons between what they have learned in the classroom and what they are doing in practice. In such cases, it would be worthwhile to encourage students to interact with each other, and see if any- one has vastly similar or different experiences.

If students work too independently, then the class will take on the tone of a one-on-one type correspondence course and will lack the potentially exciting group dynamic. To encourage interactive discussion, the instructor should make every student feel recognized and included, by responding quickly to comments and acknowledging students by name when referring to their contribution. As Blankespoor (1996) advises, "The key to reducing or eliminating bias about students is to take a personal interest in every student."

I do not think it is necessary for the instructor to answer each student individually, as if playing several games of ping-pong, one with each student; instead, it is more meaningful to respond to several students at a time, weaving together the similarities and differences in their responses and moving the analysis to a deeper and more profound level by asking new questions generated from the discussion. I think it also helps students enormously if your responses are positive in tone. Always try to draw on their strengths and build on them. If you disagree with them or feel that they have been incorrect, then correct them with tact, pointing out the positives in what they have said before giving suggestions for improvement, as online critiques can sound much harsher than perhaps intended as they are devoid of voice inflections and facial expressions.

We have talked about the advantages for students to be active learners, but there is also a pragmatic reason as to why it is advantageous to read responses from students throughout the semester. For example, if two students both turn in a brilliant final paper, yet one participates actively throughout the semester while the other is mostly absent from discussion, how can you determine the authenticity of the second student's work or feel that this student is equally deserving of an A?

Are Personality Traits of Introversion/Extroversion Altered by Communicating Online?

I find it quite interesting to ponder as to whether certain behaviors, such as being naturally extroverted or introverted, are altered by communicating online rather than face to face. I wonder also about the consequent impact on the dynamics of the group as a whole. How many students are terrified by the seemingly indelible quality of their response, which, once submitted, is there for all to see? In other words, how many students are "cyber shy"?

I would argue that there are, in fact, many reasons why normally shy students in the campus class have greater opportunities for online participation. Many of the following constraints, which naturally exist in a face-to-face environment, are lifted.

Freedom from Spatial Constraints

In the campus class, we are sometimes restricted by the seating arrangement, especially in those classrooms that are oddly shaped or have built-in furniture; and often on campus, it is those students who occupy front row seats who participate the most.

Many instructors, often unconsciously, are positively prejudiced toward the best students, which raises the interesting question as to whom do we teach? Blankespoor (1996) states, "Most of us like to interact with those who are doing well in our class." It is gratifying and exciting, so it might well be the case that our eyes look more frequently to our brightest students, as it is from them that we receive the most encouragement and are likely to receive the best answers to our questions. We might, therefore, be allowing our favorites to dominate the discussion.

We should not ignore a whole section of our class—possibly the very students who need us the most or who have something to contribute but shy away instead. (Brookfield and Preskill, 1999). I believe that conditions are more egalitarian online, because everyone has an equal chance to participate.

Freedom from Temporal Constraints

The online class is available 24×7. In this way, when you or your students have a good idea or generally feel inspired, you know the class is available and receptive. We might not necessarily feel our best at the scheduled time that a class meets on campus, but online we can join our class with a flick of a switch, as soon as we have an inspiration, thereby grabbing the idea while it is fresh and exciting.

This also helps the less assertive students who might not have had the time to respond in the finite time frame of the campus classroom as others talked first, talked more loudly, or generally interrupted them. It also helps to alleviate situations that can arise on campus in which you, the professor, ask a question and because there is no ready response and because the silence makes you uncomfortable, you provide the answer. Online students have more time to be reflective and provide well-thought-out answers.

Being online also helps to alleviate those awkward situations that can arise on campus, in which a student asks a question that stumps you. Instead of resorting to saying, "Good! Let's discuss that next week," you can research the answer there and then, and log back on with an informative response.

On campus it is advisable to create a smooth transition from one class to the next by starting the new class with questions about the previous one, such as, "What are some of the most important points we learned last week?" or "What surprised you most from last week?" (Brookfield and Preskill, 1999). Transitions are of less concern online because there are no discreet time intervals between classes. In fact, you can continue to have discussion about a previous topic, even as you open a new forum to consider the next topic.

I should also add that even though this is an asynchronous model and students log on at their convenience, you still want to move them along to new topics as a group, to ensure meaningful interactivity.

Freedom from Cultural Constraints

Different cultures have different norms of what is considered respectful behavior. For example, Americans consider good eye contact to be of importance to demonstrate active listening, whereas other cultures consider a person to be more respectful when demure and distant from the professor. This latter type of response can be misinterpreted in a campus class here in the United States, but these kinds of confusions do not exist online.

We must be mindful, however, of the design of our online class, in terms of language and graphic representations, so that students of other countries do not feel confused. A U.S. mailbox, clearly understood by American students as representing e-mail, can look like a rubbish bin to students of some other cultures (Cassidy, 2002). Generally speaking, though, students of various cultures enjoy the increased opportunities that online discussion allows.

Some Obstacles to Participation in Online Discussion

Despite freedom from the constraints mentioned, there can still be inadequate participation in online discussion in some classes. We should first consider what is meant by silence online. Brookfield and Preskill (1999) tell us not to fear silence, although they are making this comment in reference to the campus class. I know from my own campus teaching, or observation of courses on campus, that a question thrown out to the students only to be met by silence is a pretty scary thing, and often gives the instructor the feeling that things are not going well. Often the instructor overcomes the discomfort by filling in the silence and answering the question instead of waiting to see if a student will do so. I think, on campus, it is important to remember that silence does not necessarily mean a lack of student interest, but could, instead, mean that students are thinking and constructing their ideas, and what the instructor should do to allow time for thought is to perhaps rephrase the question. But what does this mean online? What is silence online? It could be defined as no new responses after a significant amount of time, such as a day perhaps, or even half a day, if it is a large class.

Richardson and Turner (2001) concluded, after sampling online courses in their university, that effective communication cannot happen online, as it leads to fragmentation and isolation of all online participants. According to them, students reported missing the "visual, kinesthetic and sound cues that facilitate communication." One student said, "It seems unnatural that we have to think about what we want to say, rather than just saying it." In regard to this particular student, I cannot help wondering if he or she does not feel some necessity to think before speaking as well. Richardson and Turner (2001) report that another student said he was uncomfortable that, after having posted a comment, no one responded to it, but instead the conversation "dragged on without anything useful being said." Let us investigate why students might not be participating, apart from experiencing technical problems, and then let us look at what can be done to improve the situation.

I would like to suggest the following reasons why certain students are not participating in an animated online discussion.

- The absence of visual and oral cues can initially confuse some students (Rohfeld and Hiemstra, 1995).

- The asynchronous format could make the discussion feel disjointed if there is a time lag between responses (Rohfeld and Hiemstra, 1995).

- They are not highly motivated students. A student might feel moved by certain responses, but nevertheless, for reasons of time constraints, laziness, discomfort, or possibly inertia, remains silent.

- Your class has not engaged them, perhaps because your questions are too vague, or your class does not yet feel safe to them.

- Students are confused by the tangled threads of the threaded discussion format. At best, they can only see the immediate message to which they are responding, but what about the buildup of conversation leading to this last response? And, if they read through all new responses before adding any responses of their own, they might be lost and unable to find their way back to the key messages to which they wanted to respond.

- Student postings are excessively long and therefore create a disincentive for discussion.

- Some students might not own computers, and are therefore at a disadvantage, as they might need to endure long waits for an available machine in a computer lab, whereas those who own a computer can happily click into their class at any time.

- If the class is relatively large, and if you have required students to respond in every forum, is this possibly introducing an artificial element into the normal evolution of conversation? In the traditional class, does every student join in with discussions on every topic? If there are over twenty students, for example, might it become repetitive, as there is nothing original left to say about a topic?

Suggestions for Overcoming Lack of Participation

I would like to turn attention to what can be done to stimulate a hearty, intelligent discussion. As Dan Eastmond stated in 1992, "A healthy computer conference carries an aura of excitement. The topics are engaging, comments build upon each other, and everyone participates." A thoroughly involved and interactive discussion is desirable because it is an important pedagogical tool that helps to promote thinking (Berge and Muilenburg, 2002). I believe that it is not inevitable that communication becomes fragmented and students feel isolated in the online setting, as Richardson and Turner stated. Many online students reported that they became better acquainted with their classmates online than in any campus classes. They also said that they disclosed information of a much more personal nature than they could imagine sharing in a face-to-face situation. But how can we promote the conditions for all students to want to participate? I think this can be done in the following ways.

Circumvent Problems before They Occur

If you are teaching a hybrid class, students should be clear from your course description that the course will include a Web component. I would advise that students be told they need a computer if they want to take a hybrid or a fully online course. Studies are increasingly showing that students who do not own a computer enjoy the online class less than those who own one (Benson and Wright, 1999), although certain exceptions apply—one of the most enthusiastic students in my online class does not own a computer.

At registration, students also should be informed that if they are taking an online course, it is not a "soft option"; the course requires independence and maturity in reaching goals. It might also be fair and honest to let students know that participating in an online class takes more, not less, time than a class on campus.

Ask the Right Questions

Asking the right questions is crucial in stimulating a good discussion. In fact, Berge and Muilenburg (2002) state: "In a constructivist learning environment, the instructor always needs to keep in mind that when facilitating online discussion, asking the right questions is almost always more important than giving the right answers."

Design High-Level Questions

You should attempt to promote the right conditions for constructive thinking in the online class. As mentioned in Chapter 3, this is thinking that (1) constructs knowledge from personal experience and prior learning, and (2) subsumes concept formation, creative problem solving, and shared social meaning through collaboration among the class group. In so doing, you should attempt to design high-level questions that are as interesting as possible, with topics that are controversial, and stimulate thought and a variety of ideas. In other words, your aim should be to make the class an incredible experience, one that the student would not want to miss.

Many types of good questions can initially stimulate online discussion. They can be thought provoking and hypothetical (if you were _____, what would you see?) or evaluative (what do you think is better, x or y?). They could tie into whatever is topical at that point in time. They can be controversial. They can involve a case study, role-play, or synthesis of elements already learned (Berge and Muilenburg, 2002).

Types of Questions to Avoid

Avoid asking questions that are too vague. If the class has not yet become a safe place, an open-ended question such as "What do you think?" or "Who wants to start us off?" or, "Are there any questions" could be met with no response (Brookfield and Preskill, 1999). I think this might especially be the case in the online class, when at the beginning of the semester every aspect of the class feels so new. A student might fear asking a question, in case it seems too stupid, and then the stigma seems indelible.

Avoid questions that require a yes or no answer or that ask for one specific fact. I once worked with a history professor who asked questions such as, "When was the Battle of Waterloo?" and then was disappointed that he had very little student participation. So he redesigned his class to include higher order questions that, given certain facts, asked students to make comparisons, make predictions, suggest causes. This provoked constructive thought and opened the gates for meaningful discussion. Avoid, too, asking students for their opinion, as this is a lower order of thinking; but if the student is asked to substantiate why he or she feels this way, this would entail constructive thought.

Encourage an Informed Conversational Style

One thing to warn against is student postings that are too long and sound more like essays than informed conversational remarks, as this makes them harder to respond to than in a face-to-face discussion in which interruptions or rebuttals are more common, stimulating, and expected. This definitely points to the advantage of keeping postings succinct and informal, because if they are excessive in length they are not likely to be critiqued, implying that students would gain knowledge by accumulation instead of by argumentation (Wegerif, 1998).

Encourage Conversational Development
with Full Participation

Perhaps not every student can answer every original question posed by the instructor and still contribute an original thought. My hope is, though, that the conversation resulting from the original question will lead in many exciting directions, so that every student will feel inspired to contribute to discussion at some point. Berge and Muilenburg (2002) feel it is important, if discussion is thriving among the students, for the instructor to step back, and let it happen. Then when things start to wane, the instructor can either weave together different student remarks to summarize what has been said, or "give up the chalk" (Patenaude, 1999), which translated into the online context means letting students do the weaving of discussion threads.

Even if the instructor weaves and summarizes, this does not have to be the final answer. From this summary more questions can emerge, prompting the students to explore the topic yet more deeply. Examples of good follow-up questions include: What reasons did you have for saying this? Can you please elaborate? How do you define x? What do you think might be the implications of your previous statement? Are there any alternatives to this approach? (Berge and Muilenburg, 2002). In this way, the instructor ". . . nurtures the conference to accomplish objectives and create a productive experience for all participants" (Rohfeld and Hiemstra, 1995). This pivotal stage, which Salmon calls "Knowledge Construction," is vital for collaborative learning. She provides a nice quotation from Rowntree, who in 1955 wrote in the *British Journal of Educational Technology*, "What [students] learn, of course, is not so much product (e.g. information) as process—in particular, the creative, cognitive process of offering up ideas, having them criticized or expanded on, and getting the chance to reshape them (or abandon them) in the light of peer discussion. The learning becomes not merely active, but also interactive" (quoted in Salmon, 2000). In this way, students are more involved with knowledge construction than knowledge dissemination.

Ask the Students to Become Discussion Leaders

An interesting option to try later in the semester is that instead of the instructor asking questions from the readings, the students are asked to develop discussion questions. To assist them in asking pertinent questions, the instructor can tell the students to imagine that the author of the piece they are reading is going to visit the class and ask them what questions they would like answered. The students are encouraged to read critically and look for omissions, unsupported assumptions, and so on (Brookfield and Preskill, 1999). I think this activity can work nicely online. If the class is relatively small, each student can evolve a few questions; but in larger classes, group work may be beneficial. Students can compare questions asked and look for commonalities and differences. They can then think about ways in which they could respond to these questions.

Ask Students to Complete the Sentence

The activity of completing a sentence is another means to stimulate discussion. This idea was mentioned as an icebreaker activity in the "Virtual Lounge" of your class, as a way to encourage students to become acquainted, but it can also be used for discussion of course-related materials. You could initiate discussion with a sentence such as, "What most struck me about the book we are reading is . . ." Once the students (either working individually or in groups) post their completed sentences, they are ready to begin discussion by asking each other about responses that have captured their interest (Brookfield and Preskill, 1999).

Playing Devil's Advocate

We cannot forget the idea of playing devil's advocate, which can be fun and work effectively online. This activity helps students to consider things from a different perspective and learn how to substantiate an opinion. One useful technique by which students can substantiate an opinion is to ask them to find relevant quotations to illustrate important parts of their reading or affirm or challenge the points made.

Consider the Layout of Responses

Is the way the responses are displayed on the discussion board a disincentive for contribution? This, of course, depends on the software program used, but I think with a threaded discussion layout, as opposed to laying out responses in chronological order, there is the potential for some confusion to arise. I also think there is the very real danger of a student not reading all the responses, especially if this student has not logged on for some time, and now is faced with an overwhelming number of new responses. We want students to read everything, to make sense of the discussion as a whole, and truly to replicate what happens in the traditional classroom, where presumably everyone hears everything that is said.

If you are using a software program that has a threaded discussion layout, I have a few suggestions that you and your students can use to make conversation strands easier to comprehend.

- Change the title of your message to a few words that capture and reflect what you are saying. This will provide a clear and easy reference for readers.

- Mention people by name and give a brief synopsis of what they said before responding, so that it is clear to which response, or even which part of which response, your message is referring. In other words, do not post, "Yes, that's true!" because when read in isolation as a new response it makes little sense and does not stand alone. Formulate a response such as, "Yes, Bill. When you mentioned that ethics in the workplace is sliding, I agree, as I see a huge increase in cut-throat competitive practices."

- When opening a new discussion forum, do not ask many questions within one message, but post a separate message for each question. If an instructor asks, for example, three separate questions all in one posting, the students are likely to answer all the questions within one response, which would make that response extremely long. We all know that a response that spans several screens is daunting, puts many people off reading it, and is not conducive to discussion. If posted separately, however, each question forms the start of a separate thread of a discussion, and student answers will be shorter as they will only be addressing one question at a time. This practice will increase the likelihood of interaction and continued discussion.

- Many software programs have a search function, which you can use either to search for a particular person or a keyword or phrase. It will then display all responses containing the name or word(s) you requested.

Be Encouraging to Students Who Remain Quiet

If you have tried these strategies and the student is still not participating, then you could try to lure him or her into the discussion forum, never by nagging, but instead trying to encourage responses by a friendly word privately expressed through e-mail, phone, or in person. Remember that students have a variety of learning styles and so might feel comfortable with different activities and at different rates. Furthermore, repeat students might more quickly establish a level of comfort, and they might either assist or intimidate students who are taking their first online class. I suggest that you refrain from calling on a particular student or students who have been quiet for some time, as the objective is not to embarrass anyone, and, furthermore, they might not be online to see they are being called.

A few students might continue to hold back and barely participate, even after you have sent encouraging e-mails or made enthusiastic phone calls. As Fisher (2001) asks, how much should you continue to try to encourage a quiet student to participate? Does this expose the student's lack of knowledge causing him or her psychological harm, or will it enhance learning? Practically speaking, if students continue not to participate and prefer to "lurk" (a word I actually dislike, as to me, it conjures up images of men in dark alleys, wearing raincoats with collars turned up), should we continue to do anything about this? After all, are not our students responsible, mature adults who should be aware of the consequences, as long as you have spelled out your expectations and requirements at the start of the class? If a student did not appear in the traditional classroom, would we be as concerned? Why should this be different?

For most students, though, free of many of the constraints of the campus class, the online environment truly pushes back the classroom walls. Even the students who are hesitant to participate in online discussion because of fear of poor writing skills grow to appreciate that good written communication is important to every aspect of their lives; and the more practice they have at writing, the better they become at it. Furthermore, whereas in a campus class, the spoken word can evaporate into the air, the online class, by contrast, has a perfect written record of all that has transpired. In this way, every student has a complete and thorough set of class notes.

Fluctuations in Rates of Participation

Do not be worried if participation in online discussion lags at certain points of the semester. This could be due to a holiday or midterms. I have sometimes found that a lag in participation occurs about two-thirds of the way through the course. At the beginning students have a lot of energy, especially because they are inquisitive about the newness of the environment, then there is continued high participation as everyone becomes familiar with communicating this way, and then, before the push toward the end of the semester, students sometimes seem to fall away a bit. There are various methods by which you can revitalize your course, and these will be looked at in more depth in Chapter 7.

How We Speak Online

Just as it is said that our eyes are the windows to our soul, then maybe it is fair to suggest that our words are the windows to whom we are online. This is especially true if we only teach online and never meet the students, but even if we do meet with them on campus as well, our words are what convey who we are when we are interacting online.

Style of Online Writing

For us, as teachers, I would like to suggest that there are two different styles of writing. There is our more formal style, which we employ in our lectures; and there is the other style, the one that breathes life into the course and sustains it throughout the semester, and this is our voice in the discussion forums. As academicians, I think we are probably all used to writing formal pieces of work, and for these we might well compose in our word processors, with its barrage of tools such as spell and grammar check. The other type of writing within the discussion forums is new to some of us. It is the quotidian writing of asking questions, responding to student comments, and asking more questions. This conversational writing style mimics the way I would speak if I were sitting with my students in a seminar. It is for this reason that I compose my words directly online, as opposed to first typing in the word processor, as I want the immediacy, the excitement, and not the psychological jarring of switching between computer programs.

Is There a Relaxation of Standards?

Most of us have come across e-mails, even some sent by fellow acade-micians, in which there is a tremendous relaxation of the usual rules of spelling and grammar. E-mails are generally sent off quickly, as often there is a felt need to respond promptly, which could account for some of the casualness of style. In a captivating interview on New York's Public Radio WNYC (December 2001), Brian Lehrer, the host, asked Dr. David Crystal, Honorary Professor of Linguistics at the University of Wales, and author of the new book, *Language and the Internet*, whether the Internet is responsible for "ripping the English language to shreds." Should we be pitying the English language, Lehrer asked, since, on the Internet, complete sentences are reduced to three-word phrases, "capitalization is dying on the vine," and not many people use formalities such as "Dear" when they write to each other?

Crystal argued that far from depleting our language, the Internet has enriched, extended, and enlivened it. He said that with the intro-duction of any new technology, people are initially a little worried, as no one wants to make a change, and it is a break with the familiar. Therefore, people pay extra attention when using it, and they make concerted efforts to make it work for them. He drew an analogy with the rise of broadcasting in the 1920s, saying that people were fearful then that language would be detrimentally affected, yet conversely it has grown since then. The same, he feels, is true of the Internet.

Writing on the Internet Is in a Constant State of Flux

Prior to the availability of the Internet, Crystal said, people had two main ways of communicating: by speech or by writing. He feels that the Internet provides an extra new and exciting dimension. He said that it is not like writing, because if you are reading a written book and decide to stop at page 10, you know you can return to page 10 and it will remain the same. With the Internet, however, things are in constant motion. If you stop at a particular screen and return later and refresh it, things will have possibly changed, as the Internet is animated and dynamic rather than fixed and static.

Crystal said the Internet is like speech—it can be either formal or informal, depending on the relationship between speaker and listener.

He added that the Internet can presuppose quite an intimate forum of exchange, and as such there can be more of an elliptical construction of word usage, and the users "can get away with it." Similarly, he has seen, as I am sure we have too, some very long sentences and messages on the Internet.

Language, according to Crystal, is our means of communication, and the Internet lets us do just that all the time. It can be convenient and flexible, and can even allow us to speak to many people at the same time, not only as in a group e-mail, but also in an online class.

Online Expression of Emotions

During the broadcast, the subject of how to express emotions was introduced, because we are devoid of body language, facial expression, and tone of voice when we communicate on the Internet. It was noted that people generally use more exclamation points and that the colon and semicolon are in danger of becoming an "endangered species." There is also a growing usage of emoticons such as smiley faces. Crystal was asked why smiley faces had not been used before the Internet, and he answered that written language has its equivalents in the exclamation point or question mark, developed hundreds of years ago. He said these were the attempts, then, to capture the melody and inflexion of the speaking voice, and compensate for what letters alone could not convey. He also said that emoticons (which I must admit I do not like) are not used extensively. In a huge sample of e-mail messages that he analyzed, less than 10 percent used them.

New Internet Words and Abbreviations

Interestingly, about 2,000 new words have been introduced since the Internet came into existence, such as putting "e-" in front of words, or "dot com." There are also amazing abbreviations that have evolved. I was musing about a humorous online exchange I had with my niece who is in England. We were using Instant Messaging, so this was taking place in real time, and I had made an off-the-cuff remark and had received back from her the perplexing message "LOL." When I asked her to explain what that meant she replied with the even more perplexing, "ROFL." My teenage sons translated for me, and if you are as intrigued as I was, let me enlighten you: LOL means "laughing out loud" and ROFL means she had reached such a high degree of hilarity that she was "rolling on the floor laughing." Other examples of abbreviations are X!, meaning "typical woman," and Y!, meaning "typical man." What is most incredible, however, in terms of the Internet, is the sheer rapidity with which new words are diffused among the population. Crystal said that because of the profusion of electronic connections, a new word can go round the language faster than anything in linguistic history.

Is the Language of the Internet Robbing Us of Our More Complex Language Structure?

Lehrer asked Crystal if, in all these ways, the Internet is creating a mass popular language, and is indeed robbing children of knowing and using a more complex language structure. Crystal answered that he conducted a study of school children to investigate whether they would think that it was so "cool" to communicate in the way they do on the Internet that they would apply it to all other social settings. But he found that this was not the case, and that in the classroom they spoke in a more sophisticated manner. Crystal's conclusion, therefore, is that not only does the Internet not lower standards of language in general, but also that it widens the range of stylistic abilities that children and indeed older people have previously had.

A logical next question, then, is what happens when that class exists on the Internet? I do not know if Crystal has studied this, but I can say from my experience that it seems, in the vast majority of cases, that the fact that it is a classroom supercedes the fact that it is being held on the Internet. Seldom have I seen students relax academic standards of articulation and expression. I have seen a small sprinkling of emotions, but generally that is the extent of it.

The Importance, for the Instructor, of Being a Role Model for Standards of Writing

Even though we want spontaneity and a conversational tone, I think messages should be reviewed before posting. They should again be reviewed immediately after posting, and any changes can be made using the edit button. I have heard some instructors lament the absence of spell check in the online setting, but I personally believe that spell check is never enough as work needs to be read through. "Witch way? Write over their" would be ignored by spell check (though the grammar check might pick this up).

Why do I suggest this time-consuming exercise of reading and rereading our responses when posting, when we all know that teaching online already takes a long time? I recommend it because the instructor is the role model for the students. How will students feel about an instructor who makes spelling mistakes, or whose sentence does not make grammatical sense? In the first place, reading a response containing plenty of mistakes can detract from the sense of the message. Then there is the danger that the students' respect for that instructor might decrease. Obviously, the occasional mistake can slip by unnoticed, and also I do not mean to suggest that the writing within the discussion forum should become laborious and lose its spunk and spontaneity. Keep it sounding like you. Remember too that you, as instructor, also set the tone. If your work appears sloppy to students, how can you expect much but sloppiness back from them? Or perfect answers, neatly typed, with a degree of disdain perhaps? We, as instructors, certainly do not want to risk that.

Besides looking at writing style in a general sense, I think it is important to detect individual differences. For example, does each student feel comfortable in self-expression, or is there discomfort because of differences of gender, race, religion, or age, which might inhibit a student from speaking? We have talked about the democratizing nature of the online environment—how the instructor, free of visual cues, reads each student response equally and with an unbiased approach. But, what of the students themselves? Since they are disembodied, do they lose inhibitions which they might experience in the traditional classroom?

Scope for Misinterpretation

We need to be mindful of how our words might be interpreted, although sometimes it is impossible to anticipate every pitfall. One student mentioned how sad she was when she wanted to thank her mother for having sent her a gift, yet her mother read her words, "Thanks a lot," as being sarcastic, as if implying that she hated the present. An instructor bemoaned a situation in which she sent back a piece of work, and her word "resent" was misunderstood to mean that she felt resentful, rather than that she "re-sent" the work.

Critiquing Work

I think it is important, if critiquing a student's work, to remember that without facial expressions and voice inflections, criticism of work can sound rather harsh when laid out in text. Therefore, critiques should be handled tactfully by mentioning the positive points before making suggestions for change and improvement. In this way, the critique should be seen as helpful and constructive, rather than demeaning. And, if you are teaching a class in which you invite students to critique each other's work, advise them to follow these same guidelines.

Using Humor Online

Humor can reduce stress and help students to feel comfortable to respond. It can minimize frustration and promote a healthy atmosphere in which to enhance learning and increase students' receptivity. Furthermore, humor can unite students, decrease the potential for prejudice, and give the class a genuine feeling of camaraderie, as trust and rapport can result and everyone can share the universal experience of laughter. Instructors who are fun, energetic, and imaginative have the potential to motivate students and tap into their creativity. Perhaps many of us have attended a class that we anticipated would be dull, maybe because of the subject matter or the time of day, and instead felt energized and engaged because the instructor used an amusing and imaginative presentation style.

On campus, humor in the classroom can take different forms. Perhaps the instructor tells a funny story which is of relevance to the material being taught, or maybe has a spontaneously amusing reaction to ongoing discussion. Either way, the instructor indicates to students what is considered appropriate. This permits them to share amusing, subject-related experiences of their own. As we know, body language can also communicate or enhance humor, such as smiling or leaning in certain ways, as can tone of voice and laughter (Fall, 2002).

What of the silent, sightless online class, in which laughter cannot be heard and people cannot be observed? What of the fact that good timing is often crucial in relating something funny? How can this work in an asynchronous setting? I am sure many of you have had the experience of trying to tell a funny incident to someone, and, on finding that it could not be explained well, resorted to saying, "You had to be there to appreciate it!" Does this imply that the online class has to be devoid of humor? I do not think it does. Just as there can be amusing books, so too can there be effective use of humor in online classes. And just as in the campus class, it also can energize and it can unite. It can draw students to log on to the class. It can ease them over stressful situations. Knowing how one of the biggest potential problems of the online class is feeling overwhelmed by numerous and lengthy new responses, just think how much easier it would be to read good, content-rich material that is sprinkled with relevant humor, rather than screens and screens of dry, stuffy text.

Words of caution are needed, however. As we know, the group dynamic is different each semester, so something that amused students in a previous semester might promote a different reaction next time. This points to the importance of knowing your students and being sensitive to their ideas. This could be a problem whether online or on campus, but there are additional concerns about the use of humor in an online class. For example, it might be even more possible to misinterpret written words that are meant to be amusing, than it would be if these same words were heard. Furthermore, it might be harder in an asynchronous setting to detect if someone was inadvertently offended, and it might be more difficult to do some timely backpedaling or offer quick remediation. Remember, as Hudson (1999) warns, an instructor should not use humor just to make students like him or her, as the primary function of the instructor is, of course, to teach.

I recommend that you be yourself, and let humor spring naturally from your thoughts. It might be wise to pause a little before submitting your response, to anticipate the impact of your words on each of your students, but I would not recommend that you thrash it around in your head for so long that it has lost all of its humor, even to you. The goal is to create a positive atmosphere in your class, and being naturally funny might be a good way of achieving this. Remember, good humor is contagious, and if you set this tone, students might feel that they can do so, too. We lack the oral and visual cues, and the immediacy that is present in a campus class, but online we have the power of our words.

Gender Differences

Some interesting studies have been performed to explore whether there are gender differences among online learners. Blum (1999) from a university that remains nameless to protect confidentiality, analyzed 149 online messages posted in an online university course, to determine male and female preferred learning styles, communication patterns, and participation barriers, and the findings were in turn compared with results in the traditional face-to-face class on campus.

The study shows women experienced more technical barriers and asked more frequent technical questions than men. In general, they had had less previous experience with computers than their male colleagues. The study sites dispositional barriers, which relate to self-perception and confidence, and again refers to the fact that men are more controlling than women, as they tend to dominate the online environment, which, the study says, is not dissimilar to what happens in the class on campus.

Observations from my own teaching, however, have been different, although I generally have more women than men in most of my classes. Even so, I have never found that men dominated the online discussions. Whereas in the traditional classroom, male students sometimes have a tendency to interrupt female students and want to dominate the discussion, I predicted and then evidenced that such a thing cannot and does not occur within the elasticity of virtual time in the online classroom, because everyone has an equal and uninterrupted opportunity to respond. The only area in which male students might dominate, though I conjecture about this with some uncertainty as I have used it less often, is the Real Time Chat feature of the online class. It will take more observations over time to see if there is equality of opportunity for the genders in terms of responses there, or whether this more closely mirrors the behavior patterns of the traditional classroom. (For a more complete look at Real Time Chat, see in Chapter 7, "The Use of Synchronous Tools.")

As well as looking at issues of domination and insubordination, Blum (1999) also analyzed style of communication, with interesting

results. She found, for example, that women displayed greater elo-
quence of phrase, substituting a word such as *got* with a fancier one
such as *acquired,* whereas men stuck to *got.* Second, the tone was
found to be different. Men posted shorter messages, had more certainty
of tone, and were more likely to do online shouting (using all capitals).
They tended to use fragmentary sentences, such as "Hey guys. Need
help," whereas a woman would be more likely to say, "I would appreciate some help, if anyone is able to do so. Thanks!" Men were often
seen to use more slang, tell more jokes, and be more assertive than
women. Women's style of talking was more often personal and related
to self or family members, whereas men's messages were more impersonal and abstract. Women more often added tags at the end of their
sentences, such as "Don't you agree?" If a woman gave advice, she
would generally write a follow-up comment to the effect, "I hope that
helped." Women were generally more polite, with a frequent "thank
you" added to their response. Blum's findings on style of communication are generally corroborated by my observations in the online classes
I teach. However, I should add that in some instances, the instructor
cannot tell from the name alone whether the student was male or
female, and sometimes not even the style or content of the posted
response offers much of a clue to the gender of the student.

In general, though, if it is true that women adopt a more personal
and possibly helpful tone, then it can be inferred that many of them are
involved in building connections, whereas men remain quite separate in
their learning. In the women's responses that Blum (1999) analyzed,
she determined that they were more empathetic and collaborative,
rather than competitive which was more frequently the behavior trait
exhibited by men. These trends reflected those of student behavior in
the face-to-face class. This view was also echoed by Kramarae (2001):
"Computer-mediated communication is not a neutral medium. Women
and men interact in different ways in Internet classes. The patterns
from the traditional classroom (including men engaging in more argu-
mentative conversations and women in more open-ended conversations) carry over to the distance learning environment."

The implications for the online environment are important. Even if
we see similar trends to those displayed in the campus class, it can be
inferred that since distance education has a collaborative potential, this

can be made enormous use of by female learners who enjoy interaction and sharing as their primary learning style. Any women who are initially hampered by low confidence levels in their academic and/or technical abilities might benefit from having an online mentor or student partner to help them over the hurdles. The online instructor, therefore, has the job of both encouraging the collaboration between women and also the independent work of men. This could be a hard task, but it seems that perhaps students in the second half of the semester could be given a project and could choose either to work in pairs or individually.

Another important obstacle for learning experienced by many women is, as Blum (1999) suggests, "situational barriers." These are brought about by the fact that women often shoulder the extra tasks of being the primary caretakers of their children and having greater domestic responsibilities. This was the topic of an interesting report, entitled *The Third Shift: Women Learning Online,* by C. Kramarae for the American Association of University Women (AAUW).

Kramarae found in her 2001 study, in which over 500 students were interviewed, that over 60 percent of online learners are females over 25 years of age. She says that online courses allow women, already juggling home and career, an opportunity for a "third shift" in their busy days (and nights), to be online learners. As so well stated by Jacqueline Woods, AAUW's executive director, "Technology does not create more hours in a day, but leaves women—who shoulder most of the family and household responsibilities—improvising to squeeze in education." In addition, Kramarae (2001) states: "In this respect, technology hasn't freed more of women's time (it has) only created a third shift in the home."

This kind of flexibility, although it opens up what otherwise would have been harder to achieve possibilities for lifelong learning, often comes at the cost of sleep or time with the family. Although women might need to deal with their feelings of guilt that they should be doing something other than what they are doing, they are generally committed learners in pursuit of a degree for their own advancement. However, it has been thought that the more roles and obligations a person has, the more psychologically healthy they are, because if something is not going well in one role, chances are that things are better in another role (Galinsky, 1999).

Kramarae (2001) found that women particularly favor online learning as it gives them much needed flexibility in their juggling acts, it cuts the costs of commuting and child care, and it provides a realistic way in which they can achieve their educational goals. As an extreme example, I once had a student who unfortunately had a complicated pregnancy and was ordered complete bed rest. Had she been taking a class on campus, she would have had to drop the course; but because it was an online class, she took her laptop to bed with her and the only remaining question was, what would come first—the baby or the end of the semester? Luckily the student submitted her final paper on the date it was due, and a day later gave birth. This student was obviously highly motivated, and motivation helps students to succeed. For busy women to successfully complete their online class, they also need much support at home and work.

Despite the fact that online learning provides tremendous potential opportunities for women, Kramarae (2001) mentions that if a class is a hybrid, some women who truly consider their education as a "third shift" might have a hard time completing deadlines or coming to campus meetings in real as opposed to virtual time. It might be supposed that if indeed women are the primary caretakers, these types of constraints of real time meetings might be harder for them than for male students.

Racial Differences

Packer (2002) explores the assumption that totally online classes (as opposed to hybrids) "could be delivered to an invisible, ether-based audience, and so could be 'colorblind' in the truest sense of the word . . ." (p. 265). She wondered, too, assuming that this is true, whether preexisting race-based educational imbalances could be overcome. It had been expected, says Packer, that "freed of the constraints of the material body, people would embrace and accept one another for whom they really were, rather than for what they represented through their physical form" (p. 265).

Packer states that it was not intended that online classes would be blind to personal appearance, but that this was the way they started out, because, in the very early days of online education in the early

1990s, the classes were not yet on the Web, but instead were purely text based and contained within the DOS operating system. Thus, it was impossible to include photos or other images. This "deficit," however, was perceived as advantageous by the early pioneering online academicians, as they thought that this would guarantee more educational equality. I agreed and frequently talk of how the online class provides the potential for a meeting of minds, uncluttered by any prejudicial baggage.

Gradually, though, I have come to question this opinion that I had so strongly held. It started one day when I was talking to a colleague who teaches campus-based classes about racial diversity. When I told her that if she put the class online, no one would know anything about anyone else's racial, ethnic, or religious characteristics, she replied that these were the very facts that she wanted to be known and made explicit and that they should not "dematerialize." I could see her point, though thought perhaps this might be specific to the course she teaches.

Packer (2002) says, "Few people considered the fact that psychological identities develop around one's physical persona, and that this persona includes race, among other things. Few people considered the fact that complex intellectual, artistic, political, and philosophical positions accrue around race, and that dismissing its existence could simultaneously dismiss the importance of these positions." (p. 266). I certainly do agree that one's fundamental character is very much a product of racial background, and just because a person is not seen, it cannot mean that all personal attributes are literally whitewashed. In other words, it is not right to assume that we can pretend these factors are not important just because they are not perceived.

However, even at the time in which it was thought that online classes would do so much to promote educational equality due to the invisibility of its participants, there were some people, myself included, who were concerned that since participation in an online class depends in part on computer ownership, then online classes could widen the gap between the haves and have-nots. This, in itself, was not so clear-cut; whereas indeed many African Americans were less wealthy, even those who were more affluent were less likely to own a computer, according to Packer. This has led to the creation of the situation called the "digital divide."

Packer (2002) talks about the importance of personal introductions at the start of the online class, and how, as we all know, these are generally even more important and even more extensive than introductions given in the campus class, in an effort to overcome any dehumanizing effects of cyberspace. She says that since the class held totally online can and does attract students from literally around the world, students generally say the place in which they live, to give some exciting information as to the location from which they are logging on. But, says Packer, ". . . in practice next to no one identifies him or herself by race without first alluding to place" (p. 267). She goes on to say that the posted names of each student give some indications as to race and ethnicity, but there is certainly a danger of making the wrong assumptions from these alone.

What is particularly fascinating in Packer's study is she found that now that the technology has advanced, and photographs can be easily attached, some students of color made special use of this feature. However, as she also says, we do not know, though, how many students of color did not post photos, or even whether those who did posted authentic pictures of themselves. Packer conducted personal interviews with some of her students, and found in these cases that the photographs were true likenesses. She concluded, therefore, that the act of posting a photograph "seemed to be a way to express discomfort about erasing race entirely and with being forced to adopt an invisible online identity" (p. 271). It was also revealed through these interviews that students chose to show classmates what they looked like, as they thought that, "people presume that someone is white unless they specifically state otherwise" (p. 271). Packer also found that it seemed to be liberating for students of color to post their photos; that once they had done so, they started to participate actively in the course much more than before. However, I am uncertain as to what this means, as I do not know what time frame Packer is considering. Would not most students post their photo near to the start of class, to accompany their personal introduction?

Interestingly, the only other students to post photographs of themselves were students who were performers of some kind, such as actors, dancers, or singers. In contrast, those students who identified themselves by place instead of race generally did not post photographs, yet posted information on the special attributes of their community. These students who talked about place were active participants in discussion from the start of the course, Packer says, which makes her believe in the importance for students of revealing some personal information, whether about race or place, as it correlates highly with increased comfort levels in participating in online discussions. Packer sees "something liberating about reuniting with one's physical form and with revealing who one really is" (p. 272). This seems to imply that we are untrue to ourselves if we try too much to dissociate mind from body.

Although Packer is not an instructor of color, she is Jewish, and her first class was on the psychology of religion. She quickly realized that none of her students was Jewish, and she started to feel uncomfortable about the fact that she was from a minority religion and that she was the instructor in a position of authority. Packer struggled with the issue as to whether she should tell her students, and thought that she should as she did not want students to make the wrong assumption as to who she was. She said, "Still, I was surprised by my own trepidations at facing a class of 'others,' and I was even more surprised by the relief I felt after addressing the issue directly and encouraging students to share their own experiences . . ." (p. 273). Packer includes this personal experience of hers, as she states how, in Hitler's time, Jews were considered to be a race, and she felt and empathized with the associated discomfort of this. So she thought that by describing herself in terms of race, she could liberate others in her class to reveal more about their racial identities, and thus increase their comfort level in terms of participation.

On the basis of the interviews Packer conducted, it was found that most students and instructors, surprisingly, did not consider the issue of race in online classes, but those who did included American students of color, Asian Americans, Germans, and any students who came from racially torn cities. Perhaps still more work needs to be done in terms of defining individual identity in the online class.

How We Show We Are Listening and Caring Online

Who Cares? Listening and Caring

One of my sons remarked to me how it seemed to him to be so hard to advertise perfume on the television, as the particular fragrance could not be conveyed. This started me thinking, by analogy, as to how hard it may seem to "listen" online, as listening implies that we can hear, and of course, online, the only sounds are those in our imagination. Not only that, but it seems to me that listening implies some sort of encouragement on the part of the receiver of information—by a smile, a nod of the head, a leaning forward of the body—to impart to the speaker that the words are having an impact, and that the talking should continue.

Also, as previously discussed, a crucial element in encouraging students to participate in online discussion, and to post responses to which we should listen, is to establish a feeling that the online class is a safe place. According to Fisher (2001), "Willingness to take risks concerning safety in self-disclosure grows in part from whether teachers or students interpret vulnerability as a danger or an opportunity" (p. 152). But, does safety mean the same thing to everyone? As with the question of freedom, safety has a twofold manifestation. It is both *safety from* certain things and *safety to* do certain things.

In other words, the instructor should attempt to set up the class in a way in which students feel both safe from abuse or ridicule according to the rules of civility established at the start of class, and safe to fully participate in class discussions and activities, as the instructor has promoted a benevolent, interested, supportive atmosphere with plenty of positive affirmation. The instructor should, at all times, express a keen sense of curiosity about each student (Vella, 1997). In the act of free expression, however, there is the possibility that conflict or disagreement could arise; but as long as this is handled in a civil manner, it might actually be beneficial and thus move understanding to a deeper level.

Once the students feel safe to express themselves initially, it is vital that they feel listened to, as this will encourage them to continue to respond. Listening, Daloz (1999) says, "is a powerful intervention, perhaps the most powerful we have as mentors. It is not a passive process, for the good listener is always alert for things of special significance" (p. 205). Although Daloz is referring, when talking of mentors, to the teacher in the campus classroom, I believe his ideas translate to the online environment. In addition, it is not only the instructors who need to listen attentively, but also the students, who need to pay attention to each other and their instructor.

Daloz (1999) suggests that listening should include, on the part of the instructor, the active process of providing support, challenge, and an ultimate goal or "vision." Let us look at each of these categories in turn, and consider how efficacious they can be online.

Support and Caring

The giving of support can make the class feel like a safe place in which to be. Caring, of course, can be addressed to issues that range from the impersonal to the highly personal. Impersonal cares might be more likely to occur at the start of the semester, when, for example, a student does not know how to find a book, but as the semester progresses and a feeling of trust established, caring might reach down to a more personal and private level, especially if the preferred mode of teaching is to encourage the collaboration of education with experience (Fisher, 2001).

The way to establish trust is for the instructor to be attentive to each student, so all will feel individually noticed. This is so important when working remotely. The optimal way to convey to students that they are noticed is for the instructor to mention each by name when acknowledging a response. I think it is also beneficial to make each student feel special in some way. Being closely listened to and receiving supportive feedback can be rare in today's busy world, so by doing this, you provide the potential for the student to flourish.

It has been my observation, and the observation of many of my colleagues, that the online environment seems to encourage the discussion of highly personal material. I think this occurs because students have greater pause for deeper reflection when they respond online, and as long as the instructor creates a welcoming tone and the feeling that it is safe to share thoughts, substantiated opinions, and relevant experiences, this will lead to greater intimacy.

Students also might feel in part protected by the anonymity of their computer screen, rather than feeling embarrassed about making a certain remark when others are watching them in a campus class. As an extreme example, one student who took a class on campus with me and who had worked at the World Trade Center, sobbed uncontrollably when talking of her anguished flight from the building on September 11, 2001. She kept apologizing for crying, and actually told me privately after class that she wished the class had been held online, to spare her this embarrassment.

Additionally, I feel intimacy can evolve due to the fact that students are not interrupted when formulating a response (as they might be in real time in the campus class) and they all have the chance to respond at whatever time best suits them. Unlike the class on campus which meets at a predetermined time, which might well have little to do with when students are inspired or even at their best for discussion, the online class offers the possibility of continuous caring and contact. Fisher (2001) says that the traditional classroom structure "resembles ordinary life, in the sense that most people have limited opportunities for . . . talk . . . The students and I are aware of the time frame in which we operate . . . because it may become oppressive to any or all of us (too long, too short, too crowded between other activities . . .)" (p. 41). If that is the case, it can be argued that the virtual classroom expands the normal opportunities of "ordinary life," and also provides an element of choice as to when is the optimal time to log on so as not to be crowded between other activities. This can really expand the potential for good, active listening and discussion.

Generally, the caring mostly emanates from the instructor, who can project compassion. Fisher (2001) says of listening and caring on campus, "Caring requires patience and the carer's willingness to project herself into the world of the one cared for" (p. 120). Daloz (1999) makes a similar point in suggesting that the instructor can give support by empathizing with each student, and by trying to see the world as the student sees it. All this points to the fact that learning is not just cognitive, but also affective, in the sense that it can produce an emotional reaction (Vella, 1997; Fardouly, 2001).

How aware are we, as online teachers, of the emotional reactions of our students? If we are remotely situated from our students by working with them online, would we even know if a student was upset, hurt, afraid, or angry? I think we would in most cases be able to tell if we read their words sensitively and empathically, and I would like to suggest that this might even be easier to establish online than on campus, as there usually is less of a hierarchy in the virtual classroom, and the online student is apt to reveal ideas and thoughts to a greater extent than in the campus class.

I think it is also important that students are encouraged to listen accurately to each other. We have talked earlier of the quiet student, but what of the online student who writes excessively long posts which might become trite, anecdotal, and irrelevant? I believe that this could be discouraging to conversation of the group as a whole, so I would recommend advising students to keep relevant to the point, and to try to relate what they are saying to factual knowledge and information generated in the class. As long as a student can accomplish this, then I think every other student should be a respectful listener and be open to learning as much as possible from each other. They might not necessarily agree, or even need to agree, but at least they should give each other's remarks the focused attention they deserve.

The question of anonymity sometimes comes up, as some software programs allow students to post anonymously. This is especially relevant to our considerations of safety. Does it protect the students if they post their responses anonymously? First, I see participation in discussion as an important part of the grade, so this is one reason why students should post in their own name. I think much greater bonding occurs once students come to understand the issues with which each of them is grappling. It is harder to care for someone who does not identify oneself. Second, if students are stripped of their name they might, instead of feeling protected, actually feel a loss of identity and an erasure of their own voice.

However, there might be cases in which some students are fearful of the indelibility of their online responses in particular topics under consideration, so if the issue is private, a student could have the option of sending an e-mail to the instructor rather than posting on the discussion board. Alternatively, it might be beneficial to break the class into small groups, which might lessen a student's fear. What I also do in some online classes is ask students to keep journals which they submit to me privately by e-mail, and then I will select a few to post to the class. I will never post before first asking the student if he or she is comfortable with me doing this (see in Chapter 7, "Journals").

Once the student has expressed an issue of concern, it is important for the instructor to show the student that he or she is attentive to this. That might not mean providing immediate healing or all the answers, but showing that he or she has read the student's troubling issues carefully and has asked a few pertinent questions to help the student try to resolve this.

Challenge

It seems that there is an inverse relationship between challenge and support. It is a question of finding the right balance that is crucial. With too little support, students are unlikely to feel heard, or keen on learning more. And, if there is too much challenge, insecure students might drop the course. The right amount of challenge can produce just enough tension to motivate the student to learn more and think in fresh, new ways. Sometimes feelings of confusion can lead down paths of new exploration and understanding. But how can challenge be given online, especially, when words may sound more harsh than might be intended?

I maintain that challenge can certainly be given online, especially if it is done in an exciting way. This might include you playing devil's advocate and questioning commonly held assumptions, or you might introduce some contradictions to encourage students to consider a new perspective. You might even want to introduce an element of mystery in assigning a particular task. The idea of online role-playing comes to my mind, but there could be plenty of other mysterious assignments that could be done online as well (see Chapter 7).

When promoting challenge, I recommend that you encourage discussion as much as possible, as it is here that students can listen and learn from each other and thrash out difficult ideas in a multiperspective fashion. You might need to remind students of the rules of civility at this point. Daloz (1999) suggests that, when discussing controversial issues, a student should summarize the previous speaker's opinion before expressing a new point of view, to ensure accurate listening and understanding. This could be beneficial in the online class as well, and the student would therefore summarize the message of another student when responding in the threaded discussion.

Another way in which Daloz suggests presenting challenge is to set high expectations for student assignments, as these become positive self-fulfilling prophecies. This can certainly be feasible online, and can include not only assignments but also parameters for online discussion.

Vision

By vision, Daloz (1999) means that the students have gained greater understanding. He suggests we look closely at language as a clue to assessing levels of understanding: "The words we use and the way we use them are powerful indicators of how we see, of our particular vision of reality" (p. 227). He suggests there is a continuum from elementary writing styles to more "contextual" levels, in which there is varied sentence structure, less clichés, and more qualifiers such as "assuming that." In this case, teaching online puts us at an advantage, as we are in a position to more closely look at and remember the words of our students than if we were listening to them in the campus class.

Daloz (1999), like Socrates, suggests holding up a figurative mirror to students, so they could better see their thoughts and hear their voices, and thus create a greater self-awareness. This leads to metacognition, which is the students' ability to think about how they are each thinking. A mirror, in the online setting, could be virtually held up by providing the students with much feedback on their learning style. Mirroring could also be done online by asking students questions to try to further their discussion points to their ultimate conclusion, thereby providing scope for them to fully understand the implications of their thoughts.

Another way in which students can become aware of their thoughts and the thoughts of others is for the instructor to create a good role model of being nonjudgmental. Fisher (2001) states that "nonjudgmentalness is not simply a matter of withholding criticism or passively taking in the other's words. It requires active listening [and] trying to understand" (p. 37).

To achieve the condition of being nonjudgmental online, it seems important to establish an attitude of cooperation. I believe this can be brought about by an explicit concern for each other's feelings, which certainly can be apparent online. The best way, I believe, for a student to know that his or her feelings matter, is to provide clear indications that they are taken seriously. This occurred in one of my online classes, as demonstrated by the following dialogue between two students (with fictitious names).

> ANGELA: Samantha, oh no, I didn't mean to sound like I was directly disagreeing with you. It was just my opinion that the story and the outcome would have been extremely different if . . .
> SAMANTHA: Angela, I didn't think you were directly disagreeing with me, I hope I didn't come across as defensive! I was just making my point in response to what you said.

ANGELA: Samantha, I love this class so much, and I think one of the reasons is that we are so concerned about each others feelings! That's the only drawback with the on-line courses, that we can't see each other's expressions or hear the tone of our voices. I don't want you to feel bad, and believe me, I don't feel bad either, I would just feel bad if you felt bad!:) Now does this make any sense?

SAMANTHA: Yes, I think you must be right.. I am glad too that we care about each other's feelings. It's funny, but I have had so much more of a communal feeling in my online classes here. I wonder why that is.

September 11, 2001

No one might have predicted that a book of this nature could include a section on the tragic events of September 11, 2001, but I include it because it provides an extreme example of the special need at that time to care and listen to our online students. The tragedy happened at the start of the new academic year, a season usually of new beginnings, of our children back in school, of our teaching just starting, of anticipation of newness, excitement, and learning.

It was inevitable that this event had to be discussed to some extent in our classes; and I think the existence of the online component provided a very real connection between our students and us the faculty, during that traumatic time when contact with others, especially when classes were cancelled, provided an opportunity for comfort. Kempster (2002) states, "I think more than anything else that I have realized that the classroom is an essential safe environment that students really need at a time after 9/11, where they feel that they can talk about things even if they don't really understand it, where they won't be intimidated to ask the questions or express the views that they have."

At that time, in those early weeks in September, I asked myself how long we should devote to discussions of this tragedy. I recognized that they could obviously go on for a very long time, as we all needed to go through the natural stages of shock, grief, anger, and ways in which we wanted to see this settled. We could not completely go against the grain of what was occupying the primary place in our minds, but at the same time we had a syllabus to cover. I decided that we should move on when it seemed natural to do so, being cognizant of the fact that the terrorist attack was a topic to which we might return in different contexts and within different topics throughout the semester. To do otherwise would be to deny that it occurred, and this was something we could not do.

I saw so many online instructors who were frequently there with a sensitive response, and I think this provided great reassurance for their students. My own personal experience was that in one of my online creative writing classes which started immediately after September 11, students opened up and told of their experiences, fears, and nightmares; and against this backdrop they produced among the finest work I have ever seen. Their writing seemed to touch the core of their souls.

One student wrote, "I live on the upper west side of Manhattan, and see the procession of construction trucks and heavy equipment being hauled away each night. I found out I live across the street from Con Edison's 'nucleus' building that supplies all of Manhattan with electricity. It's a nameless, non descript, windowless structure. I thought it was an ABC TV bldg b/c my neighborhood includes all the TV studios. After the Con Ed bldg was photographed by a 'suspect' and it received threats of a truck-bomb, the bldg is now surrounded by cement barricades, cops. It's a constant reminder when I look out my window and see cops on its rooftop. I packed a 'run away' bag and keep it in my closet. One of my friends in the bldg (who is 72) packed one as well and says she'll put her dentures in her getaway bag each night . . . just in case . . . I never thought I'd have to think of things like this while living in America."

Another student, closer to Ground Zero, wrote, "Until January of this year, I lived on Duane Street, between West Broadway and Church. It was extremely difficult to watch the destruction of the towers, and to see how it affected my old neighborhood. I had to stop watching the television for a while after the attack. Thankfully, my former roommates are all okay, and one is living with me temporarily in my East Village apartment. We still smell the smoke at times—it depends on which way the wind is blowing."

In answer, one replied, "I have been so shocked and frightened since 9/11 and haven't been quite able to get myself back into the mindset of work and school. My boyfriend and I stood on the roof of our east village apt. that morning and watched the towers fall and then our neighborhood was barricaded and we, too, were packing emergency bags to keep by the door. The whole thing has just been overwhelming for me."

I found their writing so expressive, so lyrical, so genuine, as in this response: "Doesn't normality feel almost weird though, at times? As I cycle home 2 nights ago from my mid-town studio, down the Hudson bike path, I could see the smoke, STILL, lit up at Ground Zero. It was a beautiful night; the air smelled fresh and rivery; a cricket was cricking; and I thought, Doesn't it know what happened? The discrepancy between the horror and Life Going On as before, is so huge . . . I live on the lower East Side and my husband and I watched from our roof. I'm thankful though that I didn't see the collapse in person, I think that would have done me in. Friends of ours live very close, and saw the whole thing, people jumping and all. God how awful . . . I do have a sense of optimism about it, but am afraid it might take Armageddon to get there. One positive thing that does seem to be enduring though is my gratitude to all the amazingly brave and committed people working down at the site. I find myself saying 'Thank You', aloud and under my breath, every time I see a fire truck or police vehicle. And it feels good not to get irate with complete strangers about nothing any more."

As the semester progressed, and the bonding between us grew ever stronger, I started to see a change of attitude in some students to external events. One student wrote how she was nearly run over by a negligent car driver while crossing the road. She said, "When my friend and I walked away I reflected that even as we are afraid after the WTC, and wondering if we should buy gas masks, war casualities, nuclear bombs, etc . . . there are still valid dangers in our daily lives. I guess the lesson is—stay alert, watch where you're walking/driving these days. Our world events have probably caused a lot of people to lose focus on what's in front of them."

To which a fellow student answered, "I've had similar thoughts coming back a few weeks after the WTC . . . Not any brushes with collisions, like you, but reminders that, after an initial phase of extreme tolerance towards my fellow man, there are still some who rub me up the wrong way . . . Noisy neighbours and people in restaurants being rude to wait persons etc. . . . And learning to accept the fact that that will probably always be the case! It's oddly disturbing though to come back to those feelings when you want to keep open-hearted towards everyone. . . ."

Never before have I witnessed such bonding within an online class, so much support and caring. One student had fly to Los Angeles, and she wrote as follows: "I'm flying to LA tomorrow and am nervous about the JFK–LA flight. I've been trying to tell myself that I just can't live that way though. Trying to tell myself that I could be hit by a car on the way to work today or even that where I work, in Union Sq., could be attacked by anthrax but that I can't just stop going to work because I'm scared. It's kind of helping but I was already afraid of flying—even though I do it about ten times a year—and I just can't imagine what kind of thoughts I'm going to have on that 6 hour flight tomorrow. But the only thing I keep hearing over and over in the news and from friends and family is that we can't just stop living our lives. This is all just going to take a lot of getting used to."

It turned out that the day she made that flight was the day America first bombed Afghanistan, and I think we all held our breaths until she logged on again and said she had safely arrived at her destination, and we all gave an even bigger sigh of relief when she was home again. But her fear was real, and was manifested in nightmares that came to her after her trip, as she wrote: "I thought that I had been feeling better lately about Sep. 11. The week afterwards I had such a horrible succession of nightmares, the likes of which I had never before experienced. And after those subsided I had a few shortlived anxiety attacks but then I eventually started feeling better. You know, I flew to LA and back and was fine and even this anthrax doesn't seem all that scary. But then last night I had such a terrible nightmare. I dreamt that I was at a friend's house in Brooklyn with a really close view of the city and that hijacked jetliners just started crashing into buildings all over the city. Then there were cropdusters flying over and releasing horrible chemicals. My friend and I were screaming and watching it all through her big windows. I was trying to close the windows and turn off her ceiling fan and get a towel to breathe through. And it seemed that some of the cropdusters were spraying acid because buildings just started melting. It was so horrible. It seemed so real too. There was a strange moment in the dream too where I was running down the street and I heard a girl crying and screaming and I started looking around so that I could help her but I didn't see anyone and then I finally realized that it was me screaming. I woke up and just started sobbing."

To this, a student replied, "I'm so sorry about your horrible nightmare. I understand how you feel, I've had my share of awful scary nightmares with planes crashing and bombs exploding and being separated from my loved ones. . . . It's awful and so disturbing. During the following weeks of 9/11 I would just burst out and cry and cry. . . . I heard a young girl on the news (she was in Ohio or something) and she said that the air just felt sad. . . . I thought that that was the truest thing. *Feel better . . . we are all here for you.*" (Italics are mine.)

Tension because of the instability of world events remained high throughout that semester, as exemplified by this student's remark: "I broke a tooth two weeks ago because I've been grinding my teeth so hard at night since 9/11. I haven't had heart palpitations like __. But I have had strange pain in my left arm since 9/11. So have two of my other neighbors. On 9/12 I figured it was the beginning of a heart attack, but decided against going to the emergency room. You know, they always tell people that don't 'look' like they're at risk for a heart attack the symptoms are from 'gas'. My friend is going to the doctor for her mystery left arm pain. But I think mine is that I'm so tense these days I forget to breathe properly."

Throughout this period, what was striking to me is that the tension did not distract from the work these students were doing. On the contrary, it enhanced their efforts, making their work stunning and outstanding. I was also struck by the frankness and candor with which students were able to discuss their concerns. One student wrote that she was afraid as she was a Lebanese American, and that for the first time she felt that she was going to experience more racial profiling than her boyfriend, who was African American. Everyone sympathized with her, and was accepting of her. In short, it was a most extraordinary class, and the students, feeling able to unburden themselves when the need arose, and being so expressive and full of caring and support for each other, left room to be exceptionally alert to analysis of the course content. It might have been the particular mix of students, it might have been the time frame or it might have been the potential for intimacy offered by the online environment (we all debated the factors a great deal), but certainly we came together online to experience one of the most fulfilling academic ventures that I have ever known.

Pedagogical Loneliness

"Pedagogical loneliness," a phrase coined by Fisher (2001), describes the feeling you, as instructor, might experience when a particularly tremendous class is over. It came up in conversation with an online class I once taught, in which I could not ask for a better group of students—lively, alert, engaged, insightful—that it can be sad when this shared classroom experience is over. We had originally been talking about why people read, and from there, we talked about how sad it can feel, if you love a book, to reach the end of it. I wrote to them, "I might also add that I feel that an online class is very much like reading a book; at first you need to get to know the characters in textual form, then you start to flow along, knowing people and looking forward to hearing from them, and then, when the class is over, I miss everyone just as I miss the characters of a good novel."

I was fascinated to receive several comments from my online students in response to my statement. Two of these follow:

> I also wanted to comment on what you had said in relation to what I had said about the ending of a book is like saying good-bye to a very close friend. You had said you felt this same way about the on-line classes. I have only taken one other, and as you know, it was your last class. And you are right . . . I did feel this way! I really felt so lost and saddened when it was over. I had become so attached to EVERY-ONE! I couldn't wait for this class to begin. The feeling can be similar in a campus course if it is really an absolutely amazing and stimulating class, but this feeling of loss when the class ends does not seem to be as intense as the on-line classes.

> When I took my first [online] class last year I had the strangest feeling when the class was over. While I don't see anyone, there is a great sense of security knowing that any time of day I turn on my computer I can be surrounded by classmates and a stimulating discussion. The next morning, after the "classroom" was turned off on the last day at midnight, I went back to see if it was there. When I couldn't get past the home page I felt like my whole classroom experience never existed and it had all been a dream. It reminded me of "The Lion, the Witch and the Wardrobe" because there had been access to another world in the back of the closet. It also reminded me of a Russian movie (with French subtitles) called "A Window to Paris," where there is a magical hole in the wall of a dismal Soviet apt. building. The hole leads to Paris, but it remains active for only a short period of time, and the people must decide to stay in colorful Paris, or return to a miserable life. Last semester I decided to stay awake all night so I could watch the site "go off," and not feel like I woke up from a strange dream. I stayed up until 3AM and then couldn't take it any more and went to sleep.

I savor these comments. The first, I thought, was interesting, as this student points out that for her, the online experience is "even more intense" than the campus class. And I really enjoyed the second, especially when she said what she had loved about the online class was the "sense of security knowing that at any time of day . . . I can be surrounded by classmates and a stimulating discussion." I think, perhaps, this speaks to the point about intensity made by the first student. I also loved how the second student felt that it was like a dream, or that she had traveled to another world, especially terrific for me to read, as the subject of this class was children's literature.

That this can occur in an online class, possibly accounting for the intensity mentioned by one of my students, leads, in turn, to the sadness and isolation when a riveting class is over; but there is one comfort, perhaps. Whereas students might not always stop by your office to see you after a campus class is over, however wonderful the class, there is definitely a greater opportunity for students to remain in touch with you in an online class, assuming they continue to have Internet access. I still receive wonderful e-mails from students from many semesters, sometimes even many years, ago. We remember each other, remember even the particular likes and favorite topics of each other. It minimizes the pedagogical loneliness, perhaps.

Overcoming Problematic Situations

We talked earlier in the chapter about ways in which to encourage participation in discussion if some students are not posting responses. In this section, we discuss other problems that might arise, and make recommendations as to what the instructor should do if they occur. The problems that will be considered include heated online conversations, absent or late students, and issues of honesty.

Heated Online Discussions

Most software programs provide the facility to edit or delete responses in any of the discussion forums. If a student has posted a highly offensive remark—offensive because it attacks another class member, uses inappropriate language, or both—then this will give rise to the thorny decision as to whether it is justified to remove the response.

I believe there are several reasons why the offensive response should not be deleted or changed. First is the issue of freedom of speech. To remove the response seems in some ways dishonest, as if it were a pretense that the remark was never there. If the same offensive remark were made in a campus class, everyone would have heard it and might feel compelled to address it. There would be no way in which the remark could be made to seem as if it never happened. It takes on form in our minds and memories. So, in similar ways, I think the same process should be allowed to exist in the online class. Because we all work asynchronously online, there also is the chance, however frequently you, the instructor, log on, that some students might have already read it before you see it. If you remove it, it seems that you are falsifying the history of the class discussion.

However nasty, disgusting, and even polluting of the forum that response appears to be—and yes, comments can look harsher in textual form only—it is important for the class as a whole to try to understand the root cause of the disagreement and provide incentive for it to be resolved, rather than camouflaged or glossed over. After all, often after a crisis (a rather strong term) comes a new synthesis, resolution, and understanding. Very great insights might be fathomed if there is honesty to explore the issues. Ehrmann (2002b), in a posting to the AAHEGSIT listserv in a discussion about stages of faculty development, used the term "flaming" for when two or more students "get into a reactionary confrontation stemming from a misconception, miscommunication, or disagreement," and wondered whether it could be "converted from a hazard into a teachable moment?" Researchers in the Derek Bok Center for Teaching and Learning said, "Often when things get most hot, people are most capable of learning at a very deep level, if the exchange among students is properly handled" (Salley, Wadsworth, Terry, and Richardson, 2002).

I think this is true, but the question is, how to properly handle the online exchange between students, how to make most use of the "teachable moment." One method that Salley et al. (2002) suggest for the campus class is to ask students to step back and see what positive elements can be gleaned from this heated discussion. Because timing may be crucial here, this could be harder in the asynchronous online environment, in which a number of heated responses could have already been posted since you last logged on. I would suggest if you need immediate intervention that you e-mail or phone the particular students most involved; and if your class is a hybrid, and you will be meeting your students on campus, it might be helpful to also discuss these issues face to face, so that you can more accurately read each other's expressions and gather more meaning from the tone of voice. Even if your class is only held online, I believe it could be helpful for the whole class to thrash out a provocative issue, so you should encourage this to occur. Of course, heated and passionate discussions should not be rude or hurtful if there are areas of disagreement, but should be exciting and respectful of the opinion of others. In other words, the exploration should not be emotional, but strictly intellectual in its pursuit of knowledge (Ehrmann, 2002b).

Salley et al. (2002) also state that if a student has made a particularly charged statement in a campus class, that you stop the class and then ask students to research the implications of this statement as homework, and come to the next class prepared to discuss it. How can this be done online? Even if you log on at the right moment to stop the discussion as soon as the charged comment was made, how can you stop the class? The only way you can do this is to immediately lock up the discussion forum so that no new responses can be added, and then wait a few days or a week to open a new forum to discuss the implications of the heated exchange. I like the idea of giving the students some time for consideration, rather than just discussing impetuously and emotionally. You could remind the students that discussion on this topic should be thoughtful, and it is very likely to be just that, as we already know that asynchronous discussions often tend to be impressively reflective. Salley et al. (2002) suggest that, within the discussion, you ask students to explain why they hold certain opinions. I think this can be performed well online, as students should always be encouraged to be articulate and prepared to substantiate their viewpoints.

When a heated discussion is encouraged, rather than hushed up, as long as it is kept safe in the ways discussed, it can be a thrilling occurrence, with you and students alike feeling that you cannot wait to log back in to class, to see what has now been said and to add new thoughts of your own.

I should add that even though I would not use the delete function to remove an offensive response, should it occur, I do see one pragmatic use of this function, and that is if a student clicks several times on the submit button, so the response comes through multiple times. I have sometimes seen this happen at the start of the semester. I feel it might be in order to remove the multiple submissions, accompanying this with an e-mail to the student about what you did for the sake of house-keeping, and perhaps giving a brief and friendly reminder about the technique of submitting a response. I have found that the student is generally quite relieved that you have done this.

Furthermore, most software programs allow you to decide when setting up a new forum whether to allow students the ability to edit or to remove their own responses. If you do select these privileges for students, I would advise that you tell them that they should only edit or remove their own responses if done *immediately* after the initial post-ing. If not, and they return some time later to do this after the response in its original form has probably been read by quite a few people, then it would change the history of the conversation and could cause no end of confusion.

The Late Student

It has always been my policy to leave discussion forums open, even after we, as a class, have moved on to the next discussion topic. Many software programs have a mechanism to lock up a forum, thereby not allowing any new postings, but I have chosen not to do that, essentially because I marvel at the fact that in the online class, unlike in real time in the traditonal classroom, time can be twisted this way and that; many topics can be discussed simultaneously, depending on the juggling skills of the students; and online class discussion topics can be enriched by the contributions of new thoughts and comments.

The Returning Versus the Late Student

I believe that it is excellent if a student returns to a discussion forum after we have essentially moved on to immerse ourselves in new dis-cussions in a newly created forum, *if the student has continued to pon-der or research issues and has new insights or information.* This could deepen the discussion in important ways. In fact, I often create a dis-cussion forum on basic definitions and encourage students to return to it throughout the semester, as their thinking on the topic becomes more refined and informed. If students do return to an earlier discussion forum, you might want to make an announcement to the class to look again at that forum, as exciting new conversation threads are being spun.

I realize though, that my policy on leaving the door open on past discussion forums can also have negative consequences. The situation of a student returning to a discussion forum with new insights contrasts sharply with that of a late student who is only visiting a discussion forum *for the first time,* long after the rest of the class has moved on from that topic. Admittedly, there can be many reasons as to why this can occur, such as signing up very late for the class, experiencing technical delays, waiting for books to arrive, not fully understanding the expectations of the class (some students might be under the mistaken impression that it is a self-paced class), or just plain laziness and lack of motivation. It is important to remember, though, that on campus, if a student misses a class, that is the end. The opportunity no longer exists, if that student did not attend that particular class at the specified time. Online, however, the lecture and discussion forum remain visible. At what point does this stop being an advantage and become instead a nuisance?

A lone student responding to all the questions in a previous discussion forum well after everyone else has talked together about the issues is going to represent more work for you, the instructor (and you might already be spending large amounts of time in your online class). This student tugs the class backward when it should be propelled forward, and chances are that the other students will not even return to that forum to read the new responses anyway, so interactivity is unlikely to be rekindled at that late stage. Furthermore, this late student could just be copying the responses already posted by others, rather than saying anything original.

What to Do about a Student Who Is Late

What should be done about the student who is late? We can try to prevent this from happening by advising students at the start of the semester that their participation in online discussion counts significantly toward the final grade; we can tell students that this is not a self-paced course despite its asynchronicity, convenience, and flexibility (see earlier in the chapter, "How to Facilitate and Stimulate Online Discussion"). We can elaborate upon what we mean by flexibility, stating that some students might want to participate at lunch time, and others at midnight, and others at any time in between, and others yesterday or tomorrow, but basically everyone should participate a minimum of three times per week, spaced evenly throughout the week. It is not effective if a student participates three times on a Friday, and not again until the following Friday, because it is crucial for everyone to be at approximately the same part of the course at the same time, to permit the online discussion to reach its fullest interactive potential.

We can even involve students in formulating a policy about rules of civility (see Chapter 5). In my class on ethics, I found that besides the usual suggestions about treating each other with respect (and the unusual ones of dressing appropriately!), there was a response from one student that all her classmates keep up with the course in a timely manner; and other students readily agreed. However, one student in the online ethics class remained absent from class discussions. I doubt that he even saw that a class code of conduct was being discussed. From time to time I would receive e-mails that his books had not yet arrived, but I assured him that he should nevertheless start participating in discussion immediately, as I start the class by giving a lot of basic information, plus a hypothetical ethical dilemma, so students are not required to have yet read anything at that early stage of the course. He did not. Then more excuses started rolling in. His cousin's computer, which he was apparently using, kept crashing. His boss was being very demanding at this particular time, and so he had to work late and had insufficient time for the course. Then he did receive the books, and e-mailed me enthusiastically about how he couldn't put one book down and would respond shortly in class, but still nothing.

What to do? Give him the benefit of the doubt? Tell him to drop the class; that, through no fault of his own, the unfortunate circumstances made it unrealistic that he could meaningfully complete the course? There I was, remaining undecided, when all of a sudden there was a sprinkling of responses from him, in the very earliest discussion forums, which the rest of the class had left a month ago. I was surprised, and also admittedly rather disgruntled that I had to go over that material again. What came as an even bigger surprise to me, however, was that some students seemed just as annoyed. I must admit to not having thought about the effect it would have on them, although clearly I should have. But naturally, any leniency I might show to the seriously late student would be perceived as unfair to the other students who did participate on time, and did not have the luxury of having extensions.

Giving this matter a lot of thought, I finally came up with the idea that the fairest strategy—and one which balanced the needs of the class, the difficulties of the tardy student, and the time constraints of the instructor with the inherent need to teach and interact with the group and not with separate individuals—was to suggest to this student that he join in with the most recent discussion forum posted, and thereafter keep current with the rest of the class. This, of course, implied that it was then too late for that student to start posting responses in discussion forums from earlier in the semester, although he would have to work through this material on his own. Unfortunately this would negatively impact the student's grade, as participation in discussion counts significantly, but I felt that there had to be consequences, despite the excuses.

I believe that if a student wants to succeed in the course, it is his or her responsibility to find access to the Internet and thus to the class, by any means. By analogy, if a student is repeatedly unable to travel to a class on campus because of car trouble, then the student should find an alternative way of getting there. If it is a busy time at work, then the student must juggle the responsibilities. I have known students who have truly amazed me by having such extremely busy and hectic schedules, but, despite this, they are always the first to respond to online discussions and in a thoughtful, insightful way. If everything seems truly impossible, then perhaps this is just not the best time to take this course, and maybe the student should try again another time.

What I see happening in some classes is that whereas students mostly keep up with their readings and are ready to join in with discussions as new forums are posted, there is sometimes lateness when students are given more responsibility, such as working collaboratively with class members, making a presentation, or leading a discussion. The amount of lateness varies with the students; poor students are sometimes a week late, but even the good students possibly are a day or two late.

*Why Some Students Are Late: The Relationship
between Real Time and Virtual Time*

I have been giving a great deal of thought as to why this time lag
occurs, and have come up with a few possibilities. One is that the
amount of real available time outside the online class, during which to
get the work done, has shrunk as students have taken on yet more
commitments. Another is related to the degree of motivation, although
even students who are motivated and engaged, and who post stimulating, insightful, pertinent responses, sometimes are a little late, too. I
also wonder whether the events of and since September 11, 2001, have
distracted students, and see this as a possibility.

Another plausible thought is that the setting of due dates might seem
like an oxymoron in an asynchronous environment, in which the primary emphasis is on the fact that time is virtual; that it is theirs to fill as
they want and when they want. For, within the asynchronous online
environment, the only expectation is that participation should be a minimum of three to five times per week, at a time that is convenient
to them.

If we look more deeply, I think one definition of conventional time
is that it is the interval between two events; but what is an accurate definition of *virtual* time? Can it still be thought of as a discrete interval,
or does the fact that time is virtual make this interval much more elastic, much more pulled, lengthened, stretched, and maybe even coiled in
on itself than in the real world with its steady marching forward with
every tick of the clock, every swing of the pendulum? Does virtual time
more approximate mental time, the time within our heads, rather than
objective time as measured by the clock?

We all know that mental time does not always correlate with objective time. When we are enjoying ourselves or are immersed in an activity,
it feels to us that no time has passed, although the clock tells us otherwise.
The asynchronicity of the online environment induces reflection and
encourages one to respond when ready, when one has thought deeply,
when one feels stimulated, when one is inspired. In this context then, does
not a due date seem rather jarring?

What are we to do, because we must have dates by which activities
are performed, groups work together, assignments are submitted? It is

supremely disappointing if one or more students are kept waiting on a group project because other group members have not participated (see in Chapter 7, the sections on group work). Is it recommended that the instructor e-mail to students reminders when the date approaches for them to do a particular project? Or should this be part of the student's responsibility, to keep track, to log on frequently enough to the course to know what is expected? Should there be penalties for lateness? If so, how much leniency should there be? I prefer to encourage rather than be punitive, but it can certainly be discouraging if students are late with their own work in the asynchronous environment.

David Hoover (2002), a colleague of mine at New York University, suggests that possibly the decrease in hierarchy and authoritarianism relaxes the class into thinking that they can more liberally interpret due dates. He also goes on to say that he dislikes being punitive for lateness, saying, "I have often thought that it is costly in several ways: it puts a very heavy emphasis on the due date, so that students may come to see punctuality as more important than quality (think of the difference in quality between a B paper and a C paper); it requires more precise bookkeeping than I am generally willing to perform; and it emphasizes and insists upon the gap between student and teacher."

Maybe the problem lies in telling students that they can log on "at their own convenience." Yes, this in general is true, and is certainly advantageous in reflective online discussions. But perhaps we need also to let students know explicitly that there are, in fact, certain time obligations to be met, such as the date at which work from them is due to begin, or be submitted. Perhaps we need to be clear at the outset of the course that virtual time sometimes intersects with real time, and students need to pay attention to those points of intersection.

Academic Integrity

At nearly every conference I have attended on the subject of online teaching and learning, the question comes up as to how do we know the students are who they say they are, and that their responses are original to them. I have even heard suggestions for such precautionary measures as retina screening to ensure integrity. My suggestion is that if we encourage students to participate fully in all discussions throughout the course, we should gain a fair idea as to the caliber, engagement, intelligence, and insight of each student, so that we should be better equipped to detect any sudden inconsistency, if this arises.

Dishonesty can arise in many ways, but I will concentrate here on plagiarism and honesty of student remarks.

Plagiarism

Within academia, we are always talking and learning about new ideas, and it is essential to acknowledge at all times the source of that information. Plagiarism includes lifting information (text or graphics) from an original source without quotation marks (in the case of text), reference, or acknowledgment, as well as paraphrasing without reference or acknowledgment to the original source.

A Princeton pamphlet, entitled *Academic Integrity at Princeton* (2002), asks how this applies to the online environment where rules might be a little more relaxed and the writings in the discussion forums more informal. When a student submits a paper, whether on campus or electronically, we can define the rules to avoid plagiarism, but can the same be said to be true in online *discussions*? My feeling is that, even within conversational online discussions on the discussion board, proper acknowledgments should be given. After all, if a student was speaking in a campus class and wanted to quote something, it would be expected that this student would cite the source, if it were a verbatim quotation. I once had an online student who copied an entire online review and pasted it into the discussion forum without acknowledgment, as if this was her own opinion. But little did the student expect that I had read the same review! There is absolutely no campus equivalence to that. After all, in the traditional class, a student would simply not be able to raise his or her hand, clear his or her throat, and then recite the words of a different author, without it sounding as if the student was indeed reciting, and without, if the passage was long, the likely necessity of looking down at the article. I insisted that the online student give due recognition to the original.

The Princeton article goes on to say that not citing the source of information is one violation to academic integrity, but there are certainly others. For example, a student might be unable to find the original source and instead choose to make up a citation. Another violation is if a student submits an identical paper to more than one course, without prior permission in writing from both professors. We can also step into murky terrain in regard to collaborative or group work, as it might be unclear as to who did what work (see in Chapter 7, "Online Testing and Grading").

As far as giving students advice about how to write good papers that do not run the risk of plagiarism, the Princeton article suggests, telling students to take good initial notes and keeping track of their references at the time, which is much easier and more reliable than having to hunt down source material well after the fact. In addition, the students should be told that secondary as well as primary sources need appropriate recognition, and any words that are from someone else should be put inside quotation marks. Students should also display citations properly and cite electronic sources. As we know, it is all too easy, mechanically speaking, to simply copy information from one Web site and paste it elsewhere. Hopefully with some clear guidelines and good ethics, this will not occur.

Instructors, when referring students to materials, should be careful not to copy and distribute copies without copyright permission. If a relevant piece of work resides on the Web, it is absolutely acceptable to construct a link to it, as it is in the public domain, but is not acceptable to copy and paste it into the class.

Student Honesty

There is some debate within the Princeton (2002) article about students showing their written paper to a friend before submitting it. It can be a beneficial learning experience for both students if they bounce ideas off each other before writing, or if one proofreads another's paper for typing mistakes, but it is a violation if one student substantially rewrites large sections of the other student's paper. This occurred in an online class I taught a few semesters ago. On this particular occasion, I had a student who was a very poor writer, as evidenced in her online responses and journal entries, but then she submitted a perfect paper, which was eloquent beyond belief. This was such a jarring contrast to her previous work that I called and asked her about it. She was honest enough to admit that she knows she cannot write, and was also under a "time crunch," so she dictated her thoughts to a friend, who wrote them in proper structure and grammar (and possibly added some extra ideas of her own—who knows?). I asked the student to rewrite the paper herself.

The question of honesty within the online class can take different forms as well. I was recently involved in a discussion with some colleagues, and one of them remarked that in a face-to-face class, if a student says something which meets with a lot of negative reaction, the student might choose to deny ever having said it. This, he continued, could not occur online, as the remark would remain, as indelibly and undeniably as if it had just been said. He thought that whereas in a campus class, a student could say, "I didn't say that," in the online class, a student would have to say, "I didn't mean that."

Whereas my colleague saw this as a possible negative factor in working online, I would like to turn this situation around as an advantage. I find it helpful to have a complete record of the exchanges, and I think there is nothing wrong in a student saying, ". . . that is not what I had meant" and clarifying it further. Although a challenge, I think it helps us to seek clarity of expression, and I see this as being a better situation than denying a remark had been made.

This led to an interesting discussion in which another faculty member spoke of a campus class that she had been teaching, which was looking at the subject of nonverbal behavior. My colleague mentioned that one of her students gave as an example, her reaction to men who are always touching their genitals. When this remark was met with laughter from her classmates, the student regretted that she had spoken, and retreated into an uncomfortable position in which she repeatedly apologized. My interpretation of the situation is that it was only the laughter around her in the classroom that made the student pull back and wish that she had never made that statement. When she first made the remark, this was something she felt motivated to say. In other words, I think her remark only became awkward as a result of the reaction of others, which seemed to come as some surprise to her.

So how would this situation translate to an online scenario, in which the student making the remark would not hear laughter, and any reaction would probably be less immediate? In fact, if a comment of this nature was read online rather than heard in the traditional classroom, would anyone feel like laughing? Why did they laugh in the campus class? Perhaps it was because some students felt relieved that someone had dared to express something that they themselves had not been able to speak about. Perhaps for others it jogged a certain memory. Perhaps for still others it was purely embarrassing. They each had their private reasons, but the student in question might have felt they were laughing at her, which could be why she kept apologizing.

As I was discussing these issues, a colleague said that she thought that a superb feature and advantage of an online class over a traditional class on campus is we have the ability to edit or even completely delete responses if we find that we do not like them. I strongly disagree! Just as in the previous discussion about what to do if conversations become heated (see "Overcoming Problematic Situations" earlier in the chapter), I feel that unless a response is edited or removed immediately so that no one else has a chance to read it, I definitely do not think it should be pulled away or changed later. If, for example, the student who made the troubling response had been working online rather than on campus, and other students then started to post disapproving comments (which incidentally I don't think their laughter was about), then it would not only be confusing if she deleted the remark, but also dishonest, because the remark had been made and we should not pretend that it never happened. I think it would be better, and actually more of a learning experience, if the online discussion board could be used in such a way that students could thoroughly delve into reasons why one said what she had, and why others reacted the way they did.

I am not in any way intending to imply that there is less scope for misinterpretation and dishonesty in the online class than in the class held on campus. Indeed, it is possible that in a face-to-face situation, there are more clues and opportunities to understand meaning because of nonverbal behavior, and this can be useful information. Conversely, so-called clutter can also occur, in which prejudices might arise about a particular person for reasons of race or ethnicity, as well as for banal aspects such as someone being too old, young, fat, thin, whatever. In fact, sometimes I marvel at how accurate communication occurs at all. Just as when we read a book and co-construct the meaning of the words in front of us by bringing in our experiences which affect our interpretation, this also occurs with the written text of the online class and during a face-to-face conversation. The hope is that in both environments, online or on campus, there will be clarity of articulation and respectful follow-up on the responses of others.

Suggestions as to How to Avoid Feeling Overwhelmed

It is an irrefutable truth of the online class that it takes longer to teach than a class on campus. Of course, this will depend on the discipline, but it is especially true for discussion-intensive courses. Class size and student involvement will make a huge difference as well. As someone once said to me long ago, "It takes longer to type than to talk, and longer to read than to listen." Besides this basic fact, I have also mentioned different methods whereby to stimulate and encourage online discussion, and I have talked about how communicating online gives every student, not just the more dominant ones, a chance to express him or herself. I also have shown how virtual time is elastic and infinitely expandable. Each of these factors can increase the time spent in online teaching. Most instructors are probably already busy and quite overscheduled, so what happens if you have such a successful class, with very responsive students, so that you feel that you are constantly running to keep up? In short, you are not infinitely expandable, and just because the online class is 24 x 7, does not mean that you are.

Previously in this chapter we talk about listening and caring. I mentioned the importance of responding to everyone, so that every student feels noticed, included, and heard. But could it leave you feeling drained and overwhelmed, and consume too much time? Could it therefore lead to burn out? First, take comfort in knowing that you have a marvelously full, stimulating course, in which you and your students are benefiting from a much deeper and more profound engagement with the topic than you might have thought possible. Sometimes the very best, most exciting and thought-provoking classes are precisely those that take up the most time. Is it best, therefore, to get caught up in the class to such an extent that you do not accurately measure the length of time it takes? Possibly, if the joy and intellectual excitement of a wonderful exchange of ideas is its own reward; but pragmatically speaking, it may not be feasible.

I think most of us have experienced frequent occasions in campus classes when several students want to respond to the discussion question, but there simply is not time to listen to everyone, because we must move on to the next topic at hand. Speaking personally, I know there have been times when discussions have taken such interesting turns that I do not want to artificially restrict them, and under these circumstances, I will let them play out naturally and then have to be creative and flexible with the syllabus schedule. But this cannot happen in every class, or we will lag too far behind and will be unable to complete the entire syllabus by the end of the semester. Excessive amounts of lingering and lagging are not good. So what do I have to do under these circumstances? With much regret, I tell students that I can only hear the first five students and the others must put their hands down. I do not like doing this at all, nor do the students, because if they are involved and excited, they want their say. I try to be fair and rotate students in an attempt to ensure that if they cannot individually respond to everything, they each can at least have a say in a minimum of one topic. I might also ask a student to be more succinct when the discussion is too long or becoming irrelevant.

What happens online, however, is a different matter. It is believed that, online, everyone can speak, unconstrained by time limits or interruptions. But, is this so? It seems that perhaps the pressure of time limits is shifted off the students and on to the instructor, if the class is responsive. By this I mean, yes, every student can and might respond, possibly even several times a day, possibly in lengthy and numerous paragraphs, and consequently the online instructor finds it necessary to spend more and more time online.

It is all too easy to become totally absorbed and immersed in the online class, and you can easily lose track of real time. So often I have told myself that I will have a quick check in to my online class, and then find that several hours have passed. The usual symbols of keeping track of time are not there. Sure, there is the clock on the computer, but for me it is easily ignored in the temptation of "just one more click." There also are no ready indications of the length of a text, as is true for a tactile object such as a book in which one can immediately gauge the number of pages. There is, instead, just a scroll bar, and then any number of links on which to click. So virtual time becomes elastic, both because of the constant availability of the online class and the temptation to avoid keeping track of time by the usual instruments.

While teaching one online class, which could only be described as *explosive,* I asked myself if it was truly necessary to respond to everything every student had said, the reason being that one day I logged into this class, after having not visited it since the previous day, and found 102 new responses! In general, this class generated at least

16 new responses a day, each one long and substantial, and which, in *Alice in Wonderland* fashion, seemed in my overzealous mind, to contain a label, "Read me and Respond." Please do not think I am complaining. These students were a blend of the best I have ever had, as their responses were often phenomenal and their commitment and enthusiasm enough to warm anyone's heart. My only question was, how do I keep up? What is the equivalent of "hands down" on line, and should it exist?

If an instructor feels in danger of burn out, following are some suggestions for how to continue to incorporate caring for each student while teaching, without feeling overburdened or overwhelmed, and to most effectively rationalize the time spent online.

- *Remember to make time to care for yourself.* This is not only for your sake, but also because a less-stressed, better rested instructor (and online teaching can be very demanding) will have more to offer (Fisher, 2001). Try to set boundaries for yourself. Perhaps you can limit yourself to a certain number of hours a day; or say, for example, "Never on a Sunday" and refuse to go near your computer that day; or perhaps, if teaching a hybrid, you can transfer some activities, where appropriate, to the campus class.

- *Establish priorities and realize that it is not necessary to respond to everyone at once.* I will never ignore a student response entirely, as to acknowledge a student online is akin to having eye contact and showing you are listening in the campus classroom. It establishes a good role model for students to listen to each other. However, I will not necessarily respond to everything that everyone has said if there are a large number of long responses (I think I used to), but I will pick out the excellent, original thoughts, and comment on them. If some students have not said anything excellent or original, I will try briefly to find something of value in what they said, so as to include them in discussion, make them feel good about themselves, and encourage them to perhaps think more deeply and contribute more next time. I know! This is yet another boost to generating a plentiful new supply of responses, but I think, when handled in the way I have said, it should be more manageable.

- *Ask students to keep e-mail to a minimum.* They should only use e-mail to ask you private questions or tell you about a personal matter, in much the same way as when a campus student will come to see you privately after class or in your office. Nonprivate questions should not be e-mailed, but posted into the online class discussion forum, because they may reflect what others are thinking. By asking and answering in the online class forum, you will be spared from answering the same thing to many separate individuals, and this will save you time. The discussion forums are the energy center of the online class, and should not be eroded away by nonessential e-mails. By developing a collegial, collaborative atmosphere within the online discussion forum, you are establishing a truly learner-centered environment. In cases when students must e-mail you, be aware that they might frequently change e-mail addresses or have unusual e-mail addresses, either of which might involve you in wasting time determining the author of a message. I would recommend that you ask students to include their name at the end of their message, and also to give their message an easy-to-identify title. It might be helpful to keep e-mails from students in a separate folder, so that they do not become lost among your other e-mail messages.

- *Establish agreement as to the nature of student postings in online discussions.* As the instructor, you can model what you see as a good type of response, in terms of its length, relevance, and succinctness. Excessively long posts from online students, or students who try to monopolize the discussion by posting too many times, could be discouraging to conversation of the group as a whole, especially if they start to become too trite, anecdotal, irrelevant, or elitist.

- *Delegate work.* By delegating work to students, you give them more responsibility for their own learning and lessen your burden of time. In other words, as well as having plentiful discussions corresponding with information that you have posted as a mini-lecture, you can also have other learning activities. This would be beneficial, too, as students learn in different ways from each other, so a variety of activities might provide all students with opportunities to excel in the online class. A thorough investigation of alternative online learning activities will be the focus of the next chapter.

7

INNOVATIVE ONLINE
TEACHING TECHNIQUES

Give a man a fish and you feed him for
a day. Teach a man to fish and you feed
him for a lifetime.
                    —*Chinese Proverb*

It is important and beneficial to vary the learning activities in the online
class. A semester is a long time, and it might become heavy and cum-
bersome if the entire time is spent opening up new discussion forums to
correspond with new mini-lectures. There are many other exercises that
might prove to be effective for collaborative work, which provide alternative ways for stimulating online discussion and effective learning. As
with teaching on campus, it is beneficial to provide a variety of learning activities, to match the different ways in which students learn and
to challenge them to greater heights. Furthermore, it will be beneficial
to you, the instructor, to be creative and to reinvent yourself (Blankespoor, 1996), rather than just pasting the same ideas into your online
class from one semester to the next, as this will help the class to feel
fresh and spontaneous.

    It is crucial to provide learning activities that enhance reflective
thinking beyond pure memorization. We saw in Part I how Bloom (1956)
proposed the six developmental levels of learning: knowledge, comprehension, application, analysis, synthesis, and evaluation. In the following section we look at a variety of innovative online learning activities,
each of which lie at different levels of Bloom's taxonomy, and will
investigate how each provides new perspectives and a change of pace,
which help to keep students engaged, challenged, and fascinated by

their online course. I should add, though, that timing is important; had some of these learning activities been introduced too early in the course, students might not have been confident enough to contribute, but with sufficient encouragement and modeling from the instructor, they find they can more easily slip into, enjoy, and benefit from some or all of these learning activities.

Group Work

Most software programs allow for the entire online class to be divided into smaller groups, offering each group a variety of ways by which group members can communicate with each other online. You can create an asynchronous discussion board for each group, or each small group can use Real Time Chat (see later in the chapter), or students can send e-mails to those within their group. Some students might also opt for the telephone, or try to schedule face-to-face meetings, but the online environment seems to offer valid alternatives to this.

Optimal Group Size

I would suggest that the optimal size of a group (depending on class size) should not exceed four or five people. This size of group helps to increase opportunities of participation due to its more intimate feel. It might also be a good idea to pair up the students and have each duo resolve an issue that had been discussed in class.

Implications of the Instructor Seeing Each Group Discussion

Online group discussions are set up in such a way that each student can only see the responses of his or her group members, but has no access to any other group. As instructor, though, you have global access and can see the discussions of every group, a fact that I think you should tell your students. This should avoid any feelings of "Big Brother Is Watching You." But, and here I see enormous pedagogical implications, does your presence in their discussion change student behavior? Would this make them work more? Say less? How might it affect the final outcome? Certainly this ability as instructor to look into the work of each online group differs from if you assigned a group project in a campus class. If you did assign group work on campus, chances are that you would not necessarily be present as the group thrashes out their collaborative work, unless they spend some class time doing this, or you requested updates and scheduled deadlines for certain stages of the product. Some students might initially feel resistant to online group work, being unable to conceptualize it, but in fact it is far more convenient to work asynchronously as a group online than it is in the real world, where there are all sorts of scheduling issues to agree upon.

Group Work in Large Classes, Case Studies and Collaborative Problem Solving

Group work can be especially helpful in:

- A very large class
- Case studies
- Collaborative problem-based learning

Let us consider each in turn.

We talked about how one might feel overwhelmed in a very large class, or one that generates many responses. If this is the case for you, it might be helpful to divide the class into groups, and then have a discussion leader from each group present to the whole class. You can rotate discussion leaders throughout the semester so everyone has a turn. You can also rotate who belongs to which group, so that everyone in class has a turn working with everyone else. Whereas you might only want to observe the discussion within each group (unless you need to intervene to solve a problem), I would recommend that you take a much more active part in the discussions with the group leaders on the class discussion board.

As in all discussion forums, I would not recommend that each group representative post only once, as this discussion would be flat and not reach its fullest potential, but that the representatives in a forum should become truly immersed and engaged in the discussion topic, at times checking back with their group to discuss ideas, and then returning to the class discussion forum to continue the discussion in depth.

In addition to assigning groups for large classes, students can also be divided into groups to prepare a case study or solve a particular problem, both of which can then be presented to the entire class.

Assigning Groups

If this is a one-time project, the question then arises as to how to decide who should belong to which group. I would recommend that you assign students to the groups, rather than waiting for them to choose, as this could be lengthy online. Of course, this might be different if you are teaching a hybrid, and perhaps students can make their choices of online group membership in the campus class.

If you decide to make the selection, how should you go about it? Should you select students alphabetically, randomly, or on the basis of information you have already gathered about each student's work habits, abilities, and skills? It might be that you are likely to see better group work across each group if you mix students with varying skills and abilities, so that they can learn from each other, but some online instructors say that they do not like mixed ability groups, as they think the good students feel dragged down by those less talented, and they often feel that their grade could be compromised. Instead, they advocate choosing students who have a similar grade, as this is more equitable. This could also be determined by performing a Myers-Briggs Inventory to match students on the basis of similarity and supposed compatibility. Certainly it might be an idea to put several strong students in one group, and have them present first, so that they can model to the other groups what is to be expected.

If it seems early on that one student is not happy with her or his assigned group, perhaps you could transfer this student to a different group. If a student sends you an e-mail requesting to transfer, and the reasons seemed valid, then rather than running the risk of hampering the student's learning, it might be better to agree to the move. Feelings within group work are real. If a student feels overwhelmed in the group, feels excluded, or feels this is not the best learning situation as there is little to learn from others, this is not vicarious (Vella, 1997).

Individual Student Roles within Their Group

Within each group, as they prepare for a case study or collaborative problem, it might be advantageous to assign each group member a specific role, so that no student is idly waiting with nothing to do, or alternatively you could ask students to decide on roles for themselves. One student, for example, could be the organizer, who makes sure that the group works in a timely fashion and keeps relevant to the assigned topic. Another student could be the main researcher; and a third student could be the editor of the material, who is responsible for putting the work into its final form. This would mean that the discussion leader from the group simply needs to paste the final document onto the classroom discussion board, but this student must have been involved in every step of the document's creation and understand it well, so that he or she can competently answer questions that have been raised by the rest of the class.

The Instructor's Contribution to Group Discussion

The question arises that if you look in on online group discussions, should you contribute anything to the ongoing conversation? This should be determined by need, but if there is low participation in a group, it might be indicative of the fact that the students are not used to working together without your input, and might therefore benefit from a little nurturing, encouragement, or some useful information and suggestions from you. Also, you might want to offer some feedback or give them further questions to consider. In this way, the instructor's ability to more closely monitor online group work could create advantages for students over group work done on campus.

The Nonparticipating Student

It may still unfortunately be the case that one or more students are free riders in their group. Whereas in the class discussion forums, it is best if everyone is at approximately the same part of the course at the same time, for group work this is essential, as each student is also responsible to other group members as well as to him or herself. The fact that you can observe group discussions gives you a good opportunity to monitor how much work each individual student is contributing. It might help students if you remind them about this. The grade for doing the work might be an added incentive to work well, but I imagine that the largest motivator might be in knowing that the group must present to the rest of the class. I know of some instructors who have pulled nonparticipating students out of their groups, and put them in a new group together. I have mixed feelings about this, as I am against public humiliation and shame. I certainly think the first step is an e-mail or a call to ask why the student has not contributed to the group work.

Of course, some students do not like collaboration, as they prefer to work independently; these often are the good students who want individual acknowledgment for their work. I do not think we can ignore these feelings, as they are valid too, so what I suggest is that if you do have group work, vary these activities with other learning activities in the course, such as general discussions and papers.

Group Presentations

When it is time for each group to present their case study or problem to the class (which could be done online in the class discussion board, or possibly on campus if your class is a hybrid), every class member should listen to or read the group leaders' presentations and ask questions or make comments. It should be emphasized to the class that since comments can sound more harsh online, care should be given to making the feedback constructive and helpful.

The group work is likely to be at the application, analytical, or possibly even synthesis level, according to Bloom's taxonomy, and the reactions from the class to the presentation would be at the evaluation level, implying that group work, when carefully designed and carried out, can include high-level tasks and can encourage students to think at a very deep level.

Other Forms of Group Work

In the previous discussion we considered dividing the class into groups if the students generate an extremely high number of responses, or if you want students to do a case study or collaborative problem solving. Next, in a little more detail, we look at other ways in which students can work in groups, including role-playing, engaging in a writing game, and holding a debate.

Role-Playing

One area in which I have found that online technology holds hidden and unexpected advantages over face-to-face communication is in role-playing. This can be used, for example, to deepen analysis of a work of fiction, or as a tool by which to comprehend different case studies and scenarios, or for learning more intimately about different historical time periods. On this basis, I believe role-playing would be at the comprehension, application, and analytical levels of Bloom's taxonomy for those students who are role-playing, and at the evaluation stage for the students offering feedback on the presentation.

Even though role-playing works well on campus, it seems to fit superbly into the online environment, possibly because it gives room for students' imaginations and comprehension to soar, while being unimpeded by the stage fright that some might otherwise feel. As with other asynchronous discussion, role-playing also leaves room for students to be reflective and deliberate.

I would like to describe two ways in which I have used role-playing, in different types of online classes that I have taught. One was during a class on ethics in the workplace, in which I divided the class into groups and assigned each group a topic of study, such as "Loyalty to Supervisors" and "Issues of Confidentiality in the Workplace." The other was a class on literary analysis of several short stories, and in this class I assigned each student a character role from one of the stories we were reading. In this way, each group was assigned a different short story, and each student within the group was assigned a character from that story, that he or she had to play.

In both cases, I waited until midpoint in the semester before starting the role-playing, so that students were comfortable with each other and with the online environment. I created group discussion forums, which I entitled, "Backstage Rehearsal Area," and this was the exclusive space in which that group could prepare, for which I allowed approximately one week. After this time, each group had to put on their virtual play on the class discussion board, so that it was visible to all class members.

Role-Playing to Illustrate a Specific Situation

In the ethics class, it was truly fascinating for me to see the preparations of each group, which involved their creation of a scenario to illustrate the topic, and the assigning of roles among themselves. I present to you the following comments that students (with fictitious names), made during their preparations:

LISA: Ladies, I have a case that really happened. I don't know if you want to work with this, but here goes . . .

JUNE: Sounds like a great foundation. Another scenario we could use would be . . .

BETTY: Hi J! I think the first scenario will definitely work because our topic is "Loyalty to Supervisors." Also, we have to decide who will play the manager, assistant, and co-workers. I'm willing to play anyone.

DELIA: Hi ladies, I agree with the first scenario. I would like to play the role of the co-worker. I am not comfortable playing the role of the advisor. Can we negotiate?

LISA: I'll play the role of the assistant. I think I've played that role in real life. (smile) But after taking this course, I'm not going to play that role any longer.

What I particularly liked as I read these conversations was the way that students were relating education with experience, which, as Dewey (1938) says, is the optimal path to true learning.

When it came time to produce the virtual play on the class discussion board, each student, acting his or her part and using a fictitious name, posted responses interactively with each other in the asynchronous setting, so that the virtual play took about three days to unfold. These plays were wonderful! Students compensated well for the lack of visual or audio cues by writing in "Ring, Ring, Ring" for a telephone; adding information about facial expressions, such as, "Assistant frowns when she hears Sandra's voice"; mentioning when an actor is having an internal dialogue (something which might be harder to convey on campus), and detailing actions such as, "They hug each other and sit down at a table," or "She is drinking her tea. In the meantime Kendra (her nickname) went to the lady's room."

Although students were asked to silently observe as the virtual plays were unfolding, one student became so excited that she posted a response right in the midst of the drama, and then, recognizing her mistake, immediately sent me an anxious e-mail to please remove it. She realized that she was being rude, like an audience member who claps before intermission.

Once groups completed their virtual plays, I opened up a new discussion forum for each group, in which members of the cast from each play shed the role they had been acting, and became the discussion leaders of the topic that they had role-played. In this way, students who had silently been observing the play now legitimately had a chance to ask questions or express reactions to the topic. Lively discussions ensued, and many students commented that the role-playing helped them to become so immersed in the subject that they reached a new level of understanding, as well as being able to bring in and act through a lot of their own issues.

Role-Playing in Literary Analysis

The other occasions in which I use role-playing are in classes I teach on literary analysis. Using the same format as in the ethics class, I created separate group discussion forums for several short stories that we were reading in class. In this case, students naturally did not have to create their own scenarios, but they had to collaborate with others as to how they were going to virtually stage their online play. When it was time for a group to produce the play for the class, I created a discussion forum, entitled the same name as that of the story, and I asked each character to start a new discussion thread in which to post some initial comments—in the voice of his or her character—about who he or she is, what he or she did, and how that behavior could be justified.

Once every student started a new discussion thread with these descriptive comments, I asked students to read each other's character postings, and then, maintaining the voice of the character they are each portraying, to interact with each other by posting responses within the thread of the character with whom they are interacting. In this impromptu and improvised way, the students were reenacting the story, and many commented to me later that by so immersing themselves in a character, they had a much deeper appreciation for that character's behavior and motivation.

After allowing three or four days for the virtual play to unfold, I then opened a new discussion forum for the students to be themselves once more, in which they could discuss the story unconstrained by representing the role of just one character within it.

In both of these examples, students afterwards told me that they found role-playing to be fun, as well as educational, and in fact, students who have taken a subsequent class with me have often asked if there will be any role-playing in the new class.

A Writing Game

In a writing game that I have used in an online class, I divide students into groups of three, and ask each of them to write a paragraph description of a person, and then e-mail it to one student in the group. Then I ask students to compose a paragraph description of a place, and e-mail it to the other member of the group. Each student has then received a person description from one group member and a place description from the other group member. These short descriptive paragraphs are at the analytical level of Bloom's taxonomy.

Students are then asked to, like a collage, compose a short story telling what happened to the person described in an e-mail from one student, in the place described in the e-mail from the other student. In other words, they are synthesizing these separate pieces into a coherent whole new story. Students then post this story to their group on the group discussion forum, so that every member of the group can see it. Each group member hopefully has a fascinating time seeing how pieces of his or her construction fit into a whole new story, which provides an insight into the author's interpretation and creative abilities. Students also provide feedback to each other about their stories, which would be at Bloom's evaluation level.

Holding a Debate

Cummings (1998) has done some interesting work on online debates. His technique is to divide students into pairs, and assign to each pair a subtopic. Within the pair, one student is the critic of the subtopic, and the other is its defender. Unlike a debate that occurs conventionally, in which typically the critic speaks first and then the defender rebuts, and there might be awkwardness as to who has the last word, the critic and the defender can both post position statements online simultaneously. Cummings structured the course in such a way that he opened one discussion forum for all critics of each subtopic to post their views, and another forum for all defenders of each subtopic to post their views.

When everyone had posted, critics were allowed to cross over into the defenders' forum and make a rebuttal statement to the critic's posted opinion on the specific subtopic under enquiry. Similarly, defenders were allowed to cross over into the critic's forum and make their rebuttal statement. Students were told that a rebuttal statement should look for inaccuracies, inconsistencies, and irrelevant statements. They were also asked to include a plausible counterargument. This, therefore, would be at the analytical level of Bloom's taxonomy.

The third and final stage of this assignment was for every student to reflect on all the position and rebuttal statements of each subtopic of the main topic, and write a reflective paper, which would only be accessible to Cummings as the instructor, in which they take a position over the entire topic. This would be at the synthesis level of Bloom's taxonomy, which clearly illustrates that high-level thinking is taking place.

Synchronous Online Tools

Although the software of online learning programs is predominantly an asynchronous model, most programs also have the capacity to hold synchronous online conversations, which are commonly referred to as Real Time or online Chat. In this, all class participants can be online at the same time, and can type messages to each other, much like Instant Messaging, though in this case it is not one to one, but one to many. In this section we explore the ways in which the online synchronous tool can be used, and discuss its psychological and pedagogical implications.

It is recommended that the number of participants within an online synchronous conversation not exceed five, as otherwise it can become confusing and some information might be missed. In addition, sessions should be no longer than 30 to 45 minutes, because they demand a huge amount of energy and concentration.

Suggested Uses of Synchronous Online Tools

Suggestions for the possible use of synchronous online conversations include the following:

- *Group work* Synchronous online conversations could assist students to work in groups, if they have difficulty scheduling face-to-face meeting times. Meeting online saves students from having to go somewhere (see earlier in the chapter). It should be mentioned that just as the instructor can see the asynchronous group discussions, so too can he or she read the group's online synchronous conversations.

- *Role-playing in synchronous (as opposed to asynchronous) time*
As a possible alternative to role-playing asynchronously on the class
discussion board, as mentioned earlier, students could use their
group's online synchronous conversation area in which to stage
their virtual play. This gives immediacy and excitement to their
performance, as each student, maintaining a character role,
interacts with others in the group in real time while dynamically
creating their story. As a student in one of my online classes
remarked at the completion of a virtual play, "A challenge for me
was . . . that I had to actually put myself in the moment and act
upon reflex . . . " Another student talked about the spontaneity
and the sensitivity to each other by saying, "On a personal note,
my attitude toward my 'brother' was not planned, it just happened.
I think my two partners set the tempo. I saw their dialog and was
able to sense the mood; thus, it was easy for me from that point."

When their virtual play is completed, the instructor can copy
the archived transcript and paste it into the class discussion board
for all students to read (as they are not able to access each other's
group areas), and a discussion can ensue as to the issues brought
up in the role-playing. The writing and performing of the play
would involve students in at least the application and analytical
stages of Bloom's taxonomy, and the subsequent discussion with
the rest of the class could reach to the evaluation level. As one of
my students said at the conclusion of the role-playing, " . . .
responding in 'real time' requires a quick answer . . . no time to
think about what you are saying, or how you said it. In 'real life,'
our responses to family members are sometimes the same—said
without thought, not thinking about the effect our words will
have on others." This was particularly interesting as the role-
playing was on the topic of family dynamics, so I was especially
pleased that the one replicated so well the conditions of the other,
thus forming an accurate model for analysis.

Many students seem to enjoy this type of assignment. A
student from one online class said, "I cannot remember when I
had so much fun as doing the role-playing . . . I found myself
laughing with tears coming out of my eyes . . . I wish all classroom assignments can be that enjoyable. I felt so happy about the
accomplishments of Linda, Robert (names changed for the sake of
confidentiality), and myself that I insisted that my husband see

what was said. I had to because he never saw me laugh when looking at a computer." What seemed to be of particular value was that it truly fostered collaboration between the students, as seen by the following remarks: "I too had a blast . . . and was laughing. I didn't think I would have that much fun with the role-playing. We all worked very well with each other," and "The virtual classroom was such a great idea, working backstage, putting ideas together with other classmates, then presenting it the whole class! I think I had it easy, as the other players kept me involved by their interaction. I complained to myself that it may be hard to understand an online class . . . now I want more . . . How easy (and fun this class has become!)"

- *Virtual office hours*   If students find it hard to meet with you during your regular office hours if you teach a hybrid, then they might enjoy the benefit of an online meeting. This might be especially helpful to individuals or groups of students prior to tests or exams, as it would provide them the immediacy of feedback and answers.

- *Online guest lecturer* (see later in the chapter)   In this situation, it might be best if the guest lecturer posts information in advance in your online class, or you could have students read this person's book or article or distribute a handout, so the students could come prepared to the synchronous online conversation with worthwhile questions.

- *Demonstration of a Web site*   Most software programs have the capacity to demonstrate a Web site while being able to engage in synchronous online dialogue about it. Many software programs also have a whiteboard area to draw on or demonstrate certain concepts, while engaged in synchronous online conversation.

- *Community building*   Because conversations are immediate and fun, this could be a good way to establish class camaraderie.

A nice feature of many software programs is that if a student has missed an online synchronous conversation, this online conversation is archived, and can therefore still be read after it has occurred. This, then, is superior to having missed a meeting in physical space and time, in which the teaching is essentially lost, retrieved only from someone's memory or notes (which of course introduces an element of bias).

Faculty Reactions to Synchronous Online Conversations

Reactions to the use of the synchronous online conversation feature vary greatly. In this section I record several statements from instructors who were learning to teach online, and who were holding an online synchronous conversation with me to see how it felt. Many reported that it was fun, but hectic and disjointed. In general, they felt it would tend to favor fast typists, not necessarily the best students. One of the challenges of synchronous teaching and learning is that several different conversations can be going on at the same time, because of the length of time it takes to type and because conversations can go off on different tangents according to individual interpretations.

While typing you may feel as if you are missing out on what is happening on the screen, especially if you look at the keyboard while typing. This situation has two implications. One is the feeling that you are interrupting each other, as we are not limited to the traditional conventions of spoken conversation in that it is understood that one person speaks at a time. But this does not have the same impact online as it does if we interrupt each other when face to face. In the case of online chat, we can still follow several threads of conversation, because of the written record in front of us which we can read and reread if necessary, whereas in spoken conversation, interrupted threads often get forgotten.

The second implication of missing what is on the screen as responses fly past is that the total conversation can feel disjointed. As one instructor said, "I find this way of communicating difficult because I can't easily follow the different threads of the discussion and like now, I'm answering a question you asked earlier and you're on to something else!" Another instructor said he was about to comment, but someone else preempted his remark. For all these reasons, it might feel as if it is hard to hold a thorough and cohesive conversation on any particular topic.

To avoid this as much as possible, I think messages have to be fairly short, otherwise there is too much time lag. Also others might post things in different tangents. A potential problem of this emphasis on speed, however, is that besides there being little time for deeper thinking, there is also little chance to correct spelling mistakes or typos. Therefore, are instructors providing an acceptable role model to students if their responses contain errors in format?

On the other hand, many faculty members who trained in the class had positive reactions to the synchronous online conversations. One instructor likened the experience of the online chat to paying attention to several conversations at a crowded cocktail party. Many commented on how exciting it was, and one voiced a suspicion that once her students did this, it might prove addictive. Time literally seems to fly when conversing this way, and as one instructor said, "Does everybody know that a half hour has passed? This stuff is like a drug." To this, another added, "I think I also enjoy chat better than the threaded discussion. I'm into instant gratification and enjoy haphazard discussion." He went on to say, "What is nice about chatting is that it is a fast response. This avoids the student who spends way too long thinking and re-writing."

Student Reactions to Synchronous Online Conversations

Certainly, to some students, especially those who are involved in a lot of online chatting, this might feel familiar and easy, and because it is instant, it might provide a better way of keeping their attention. One of the instructors in the online training said, "Wow—this really is a medium for the MTV generation—so much for linear thought!"

Whereas the synchronous online conversations might fit in well with students' lifestyles and habits, is it applicable to learning, especially learning in depth, in a considered way? For example, sometimes in teaching it is important to allow time for silence, as one instructor commented, so that people can think about what was said and about how they want to respond, yet there could be limited opportunities for this in lively synchronous online conversations. This is where the more reflective asynchronous environment has a distinct advantage.

Furthermore, since many students take an online class because of the convenience and flexibility of working asynchronously, some might have scheduling problems that prevent them from attending an online conversation that is held in real time. Others might feel nervous. I heard from one student how the mere thought of a synchronous online conversation made her feel so flustered that she dropped her keys trying to rush home in time, accidentally kicked the cat, and in her anxiety, could not remember how to log on! Others comment on feeling dizzy watching responses flying past, and find it hard to formulate thoughts, type, and read, all at the same time. We must take into account, too, students with disabilities, who might find synchronous online conversations to be an extra challenge. Many students, and not only those who are disabled, might be greatly assisted by voice recognition software.

Ground Rules Concerning Conversation Patterns and Flows

To maximize the potential benefits of synchronous online conversations, and to both make the conversation flow more manageable and try to guarantee that every student has a chance to respond, it might be helpful to establish certain ground rules. Of course, some might feel that making rules about conversation flows and directions introduces an artificial element into the discussion, and limits opportunities for someone with an inspired reaction to what had just been said from being able to respond. This could well be the case, but should you be interested in possible rules for discussion so as to avoid the synchronous conversations from getting out of hand, I would like to mention what Brookfield and Preskill (1999) tried in their campus class, as I think it can be very well adapted to online synchronous conversations.

Brookfield and Preskill established a technique called the "Circle of Voices." In this exercise, and with approximately four students at a time, the instructor assigns a topic, allowing students five minutes of "silent time" for reflection. After this time has elapsed, each student has five minutes in which to type in their comments, during which they cannot be interrupted by another student. Each student has a turn, by simply going around the circle. An advantage of this method is that it avoids the pecking order of the usual, favorite, dominant students going first and possibly overpowering the others. Even though it is possible that many people can speak at once online without interrupting each other in the conventional sense, the "Circle of Voices" could certainly introduce a beauty and simplicity of structure, as it avoids the hectic, rapid typing and possibly missing of each other's responses, as the postings are hurling by.

Brookfield and Preskill (1999) suggest that once everyone has had their turn, students can react to what others have said, but, in an effort to maintain the streamlined approach already developed, each student can only react to the information of the student immediately before them, and they should do this by first paraphrasing the posting of that previous student's response. The authors feel that this has the further benefit of encouraging students to be respectful listeners, and I would add that this method would allow for analytical thought processes to occur, according to Bloom's taxonomy.

This sequencing of events, in the "Circle of Voices," allows for the synchronous area of the course to be put into good use, providing an effective and organized way to work collaboratively online. It might also be possible to change the positions of those within the Circle, so that students have a chance of interacting with a variety of other students. It should be mentioned that it might not be up to only the instructor to lead the discussion in this way. Students working in small groups, for example, could employ similar rules for their discussion, so that everyone can participate.

Should Attendance in the Online Chat Be Mandatory?

The question arises that if the instructor does include opportunities for using the chat feature, should attendance be mandatory? As mentioned, some students might find it hard to attend at a particular time, either because they are busy with other things or because they live at locations remote from the university or college, which might be on a different time zone.

In the case of collaborative group work, or role-playing, in which it is essential that each group member contribute significantly to the discussion, attendance is vital. Ideally, the group should schedule a mutually convenient time for an online synchronous conversation, and if all agree on this time, all should attend it. If scheduling problems legitimately preclude the opportunity for all students to attend a chat of their group, then they should find an alternative means, such as using the asynchronous group discussion board on which to work collaboratively.

The synchronous online conversation tool, while certainly being a great deal of fun, does not lend itself to a deep, complex discussion because it is too hectic. In fact, it strikes me as a bit of a jarring juxtaposition in an online class that is essentially asynchronous, since asynchronicity lends itself more to reflection and thus the possibilities of deeper learning. It is not completely without merit, however, and can be quite useful in community building, in holding virtual office hours, in meeting with an online guest, in small group synchronous online collaborations, and possibly in preparatory work for a project which will continue on campus or on the asynchronous discussion board.

Online Guest Lecturers

Sometimes, about two thirds of the way through the semester, online conversations start to dwindle as some students have moved beyond their initial excitement, yet are not ready for the final push toward the end of class. This might be an opportune time to invite an online guest lecturer. Just as in a campus class, a guest appearance introduces the intrigue of a new voice, possibly a fresh perspective, and maybe a welcome change of pace.

Even if you have a hybrid class, you might prefer to invite the guest to join your online component rather than come to your class on campus; and this might be preferable for a guest lecturer who lives far away or is for other reasons unable to come to campus. This will save on travel and accommodation expenses. I have had guests from India and Fiji in online classes I have taught, and it has been truly exciting and fascinating. All that needs to be done is to give the guest access to your online class, by an officially granted username and password, and explain the basic mechanics of online discussions.

The Online Guest Makes a Scheduled Synchronous Appearance

There are two different ways in which an online guest can participate in the class; either synchronously or asynchronously. We talked in the previous section about having a guest lecturer join a scheduled synchronous online conversation, and how, since time is so short, it would be beneficial if the guest posted a lecture prior to visiting the online class, or if the instructor asked students to read a piece by or about the guest. In either case, the students could prepare questions in advance, post these during the chat, and the guest lecturer could provide immediate responses.

This would assist students to reach the application and analytical level of Bloom's taxonomy.

The Online Guest Spends a Week in the Class, Responding Asynchronously

Alternatively, the guest could devote a week to asynchronous postings of information and responses to students' questions in a specially created discussion forum. This would mean that the guest might log on to the class every other day for an hour or so. Working asynchronously with the online guest might allow for a more thorough, comprehensive, and reflective discussion, so might be preferable to the guest making a one-time, synchronous appearance in the Real Time Chat area. Students might be able to move beyond the analytical level to that of the synthesis level, as they form new conclusions and make important connections.

If you know that you will be having an online guest lecturer, it is a good idea to inform students about this from the start of the semester. Ideally, if your software allows it, it would be preferable if the guest only has access to the discussion forum in which he or she will be holding a discussion. I make this recommendation because there could be some courses in which personal matters are being discussed, and these students might feel as if it is a break in trust to suddenly have a newcomer look over their previous conversation. And since trust is essential to their learning, it should not be broken.

In my experience, students are thrilled to have a guest lecturer, and similarly, the guest is generally delighted to be there, not only to teach the material but also because it often represents the first time using online discussion. Most guests appreciate the opportunity to pick up a new skill.

Virtual Field Trips

An alternative to bringing an online lecturer to your class, or maybe a supplement to this, might be for the class to go on a virtual field trip. It's the next best thing to being there! You might consider sending your students out to Web sites that take them to places of interest relevant to your course. For example, I was once working with an art history professor, and she provided a link to the Louvre, from which the students benefited greatly. In a class I taught on D.H. Lawrence, I found a wonderful interactive Web site that took us on a virtual tour of his hometown, visiting the houses in which he wrote or that were represented in his works. The Web offers many exciting possibilities for these types of virtual visits.

If you provide your students with virtual field trips, they might be better able to comprehend what they are learning (comprehension level), apply what they have learned in new ways (application level), and, since they work at the speed comfortable to them, which affords them with more opportunities of feeling in control and taking responsibility as active learners, they might be able to analyze the information well (analytical level), and synthesize this information with what they have already learned (synthesis level). Thus, students are able to advance a long way through the levels of learning as defined by Bloom's taxonomy.

Integration of Web Sites

Besides virtual field trips, the Web offers possibilities of simulations, in-depth information, and analyses. These possibilities can enrich learning and advance students along Bloom's defined learning levels, in the same way as discussed for virtual field trips.

Because online teaching can so easily link to a Web site, this can be used to good effect. I often have the impression that online students are more likely to visit a Web site that is just a click away, than campus students are if you provide them with the URL of that site. To facilitate this for online students, I think it is a nice idea to embed the link to a chosen Web site directly in the text itself, whether in a mini-lecture or a response, as in this way the Web site can be seen in context of your information. Additionally, some software programs have a special area in which to list External Links. I like to think of this area as an electronic library shelf. If you list the Web site there, it is a good idea to annotate it, to give readers a quick glance at what to expect when visiting that site.

Many of today's students are increasingly familiar with working on the Internet. Certainly judiciously linking valuable Web resources can provide a good source of information, and might mean that the students need purchase fewer texts. It might also decrease the need for assembling a course pack; and will avoid the problem of seeking copyright permission, as a site on the Internet is considered to be in the public domain.

However, some words of caution are needed. First, at the start of any course, you should check that the Web site to which you provide a link has not been removed. Some information on the Web is in a constant state of flux. Second, if a particular Web site is large and complex, I would recommend that you link students to the part of the site that you most want them to see. You want to avoid confusing them or having them wander off into cyberspace, and not returning to your course.

Guidelines for Students Doing Web Research

Some instructors also like to ask students to do a Web search for valuable material. Provide students with some guidelines as to how to best conduct Web research, as information on the Web is of variable quality because there are no standards of control as to what is posted.

First, you could inform them of good search engines, such as Google. Second, it is helpful to advise students to check the relative value of a particular Web site in comparison to other sites (Grassian, 2000). To do this would involve, among other things, researching into what other information is available; and determining the author or producer of the site, to help ascertain the reliability and degree of expertise, and to try to see if it is biased in any way. Other points of importance are whether there is contact information for the author, as well as the date that the Web site was produced, and whether or when it was last revised and updated.

Grassian (2000) also gives some thought to the design of the Web site, asking useful questions such as whether any graphic displays are merely decorative and distracting, or if they serve a pedagogical purpose. There is, of course, the very important element as to whether the text on the site is well written. Some sites are especially set up to address the needs of people with disabilities, by having large print and graphics, and audio options. Also some sites are interactive, welcoming online chats on a topic, or the possibility of doing simulations. It is important to determine how usable a site is, especially a site packed with information, as one can feel lost in a cyberspatial labyrinth, and be gasping for air and space if there are an excessive number of links. Grassian recommends that three clicks into a site, to find the needed information, is generally sufficient.

While on the subject of links, Grassian (2000) feels it is important to determine the balance between inlinks and outlinks (those pointing to areas within the site, and those pointing to other sites), and whether they are comprehensive and representative of the field. Important, too, is the consideration as to whether the links provide valid information that is not available at other sites.

Student Presentations of Their Discovered Web Sites

With these guidelines, it might be a good idea to ask students to explore the Web to locate informative Web sites on a particular topic. At particular intervals, they could each present their findings to the class, by briefly describing the site and providing an active link to it. Students could investigate each other's sites and write brief reviews of them, and by the end of the semester, they could choose the two best Web sites, and write about them, giving reasons why they found them exemplary (Cummings, 1998). Writing papers on why particular Web sites were exemplary would boost students to the Evaluation stage of Bloom's taxonomy.

Student Portfolios

Use of Portfolios in Online Workshops

If you are teaching an online workshop, you can create separate portfolios for students into which they can post their work, and then invite other students in to see this work and offer feedback. The way this can be done is that you, the instructor, can create each portfolio as a new discussion forum (e.g., Mary's Portfolio, John's Portfolio, and so on). This will be accessible to everyone, and will also provide scope for students to post their feedback comments directly into the portfolio of the work to which they are responding. Portfolios are not necessarily limited to individuals, as it might also be desirable to create a group portfolio, in which groups can present their work to the whole class after having completed their preparations in their private group area, and then receive feedback from the class directly within the portfolio itself.

Creating portfolios would be appropriate in the example of students individually presenting information about Web sites, and then other students reading and commenting on this information. Portfolios also work particularly well in writers' workshops, or in any class in which you might want student collaboration over the drafts they each write.

Comparison of a Master Class with an Online Workshop

An online workshop can be meaningfully compared with the concept of a *master class*. Ruhleder and Twidale (2000) believe that the master class concept, such as when students come with a prepared piece of music and perform it for the teacher and classmates, and thus receive feedback on their work, is a sound pedagogical model for reflection and collaborative learning. Although it is an intensive, face-to-face experience, they were curious to research the implications of applying certain techniques to a spatially dispersed student body, as would be the case in an online class.

Key Concepts of Teaching and Learning in a Master Class

From their observation of the master class, Ruhleder and Twidale (2000) derived the following key concepts of teaching and learning.

- The focus is on collaboration to achieve development of technique and skills on an ongoing basis, and is not individual work in solitary pursuit of a good final grade.

- Students are reflective of what they have learned from the group, and apply and incorporate this into their learning.

- The open collaboration of the master class helps students to learn and benefit from the successes and mistakes of their fellow students.

- Rather than learning in the abstract, students learn by doing, and this can be applied both to general topics and specific events.

- There is a process of "reification," in which all students can form concepts based on the current or previous performance of all their classmates.

Since the classes are generally taped, students can watch what occurred any number of times, which assists them in being reflective on their work and the work of others.

An Online Workshop

Ruhleder and Twidale (2000) then looked at an online class on interface design of information systems, in which students were asked to design a Web page. They thought that if this class were held on campus, the instructor would perhaps have students working individually on their designs, or would have them working in groups, but either way, the instructor would have to keep working his or her way around the classroom to look at everyone's work sequentially. If, instead, the class was to be held online, it could provide many opportunities for reflection and collaboration, leading therefore to the continuous possibilities of improving the work.

An online class was set up so that each student posted a first design draft in his or her portfolio, making this available to the instructor and other students in the class. Students and the instructor contributed their ideas and suggestions about each person's work, and what became apparent was the multiplicity of suggestions, based on subjective preferences informed by personality and previous experiences. This is not unusual in the field of design, or in anything creative. It is up to the student, with help from the instructor, to sift through the responses and make design revisions according to a careful discrimination as to the best advice. It is important that students not work over their original design, as this would have obscured their initial attempts, but instead produce a separate second, third, and possibly fourth draft, so that in this way they are keeping a permanent record of every stage of their work, and one can readily appreciate their development and progress. Each subsequent draft is also made available to the whole class.

Similarities between a Master Class and an Online Workshop

The online workshop class does not exist in real time, nor is it face to face as is the master class, but it does share many similar traits. Among them are the following:

- Importance and significance of collaboration are evidenced in both environments.

- Students' work develops and progresses, as their work is refined and improved from the first draft onward. This helps students understand that design is an iterative process and that even experts are not usually brilliant on their very first draft.

- Everyone in the class can see and benefit from learning about the work of others, the ensuing discussion and the feedback.

- Learning can be from the general (broad design ideas) to the specifics of a detail within a piece of work. The instructor can relate both the general and the specific information to actual known examples in the field, to put these in context.

- Since both the students' designs and the discussions surrounding these designs are permanently available in the online class, meaningful understanding both of design and the design process can occur, thereby permitting reification to take place.

- Since there is a permanent record of all that transpired in the online class, students can be reflective about this collection of information, which in turn can inform their choices when making new designs or critiquing the work of others.

In other words, putting learning into active practice, and seeing the work and development of others within the online class, provides a tremendous learning opportunity. Posting work into the portfolio, whether it is information on a Web site, a creative short story, or designing a new Web site, would be at the analytical level of Bloom's taxonomy, and class reactions to these works would be at the evaluative level. Subsequent revisions to the original creative piece of work would allow the student important opportunities for synthesis, according to Bloom's taxonomy.

Online classes, Ruhleder and Twidale (2000) conclude, have the potential to establish "a robust and supportive learning environment driven by a collection of human users with a shared set of learning goals in mind." I think this is particularly true of a workshop type of class, facilitated by designing the class to incorporate portfolios for the submission, critique, and revision of each student's work.

Journals

You might consider asking students to write weekly or biweekly journals, which offers opportunities for reflection on, or writing about experiences relevant to the course material. Because this would be an opportunity for them to relate a number of ideas, journaling would draw on their level of knowledge, comprehension of the subject matter, application of it in other circumstances, and ultimately lead them to be able to synthesize ideas, thus placing journal writing at the synthesis level of Bloom's taxonomy.

I recommend that you ask students to e-mail these journals to you. After reading them and e-mailing back your comments, you could select a few of the more outstanding journals and ask the authors of these if they would be willing to have you post them to the class. You could create a new discussion forum expressly for posting these journal entries. In this way, their classmates could read and react to them. I have found that this is an area in which the class shows impressive amounts of empathy and support for each other. It also assists classmates in reaching a new level of synthesis themselves.

Online Team Teaching

Advantages of Team Teaching

Many of us advocate collaboration among our students, but what about collaborating with our colleagues? After all, there is a lot of sharing of professional experience if we teach with a colleague (Cranmer, 1999). We might, for example, learn from seeing our colleague do something that we are resistant to do, or have expertise in something that we know less about, or learn about different activities to accomplish the same ends, or see a difference in priorities. Team teaching gives us someone with whom to talk about the class, as we have both shared the experience, so that we could discuss whether things are working well; and if there are unfulfilled needs, we can jointly decide on how these could best be resolved. When we talk of team teaching, we usually consider this to involve only two colleagues, but I have seen one or two classes in which there are as many as four teachers in the class. This might work well for a large class, or one in which students benefit from individual attention.

Team teaching can be extremely rewarding. If team teachers work well together, then this can be a good model of collaboration to demonstrate to students. Team teachers can certainly learn a great deal from each other, not only in terms of content, but also style.

Potential Problems of Team Teaching

Team teaching is not necessarily easy. Some teachers might dislike planning a lecture together, or being observed. Cranmer (1999) makes explicit certain points to be aware of before embarking on team teaching, to lessen areas of potential future conflict. We will discuss these in the following paragraphs. Although Cranmer is applying his thoughts to the campus class, I will draw on implications for the online teaching situation.

Concerns about Authority

In the first place, there is the question of *authority*, in regard to whether the teachers in the team have equal authority, or one is assumed to have more responsibility than the other, such as a student teacher who is there to learn some good teaching techniques. If the expectation is for equality, then problems might arise if both teachers have dominant personalities, or if either or both feel possessive of the class. At the same time, if both personalities are too deferential, nothing might be achieved, and the plans for the course to take shape might be indecisive and lacking in direction. Ideally, there should be an easy-going give and take, so that teachers can switch back and forth from being in the metaphorical driver's seat to being in the back (Cranmer, 1999).

Team Teaching Colleagues Should Be Mutually Supportive and Considerate

Cranmer's (1999) second consideration about team teaching is that colleagues should be mutually *supportive* and *considerate*. Obviously, no teacher should ever embarass another by pointing out a mistake in front of the students. There might be times when help is needed, and if so the teacher in need can send an e-mail or call the colleague. At least online there is the advantage of not working in real time (unless doing an online chat), so there are more opportunities for assistance than if team teaching face to face with students on campus. Cranmer cautions, however, that the team teachers should have absolute trust in each other and full respect as colleagues.

Concerns about How to Divide Responsibilities

A third consideration Cranmer (1999) addresses in terms of team teaching involves making decisions about *dividing up responsibility.* Cranmer advocates that for true teamwork, not only should the course be planned together, but also both teachers should be present at all times throughout the semester. In contrast, if one teacher teaches while the other is absent, this is not team teaching, but shared teaching. Online, I have seen teachers alternating lecture topics, and I have also in one case seen teachers divide up the semester so that one teaches for the first half and the other for the second half. I would definitely call this latter example a case of shared rather than team teaching.

I once team taught with a colleague, and we alternated topics, but we decided that when it was not our turn, we would have a minor voice within the online discussions on the topic, so as to remain visible to the students, while leaving the main scope for the discussion for the one whose topic responsibility it was. We decided that it was important to establish the idea of the alternating major and minor voice, because if we did not, we found that we might both swoop down on every student's response, and this could become overwhelming to the students and somewhat top-heavy. It might be beneficial for the teacher with the minor voice to also be conducting detailed observations about discussion flows and patterns, which could later be discussed with the teacher who has taken the major role for that topic.

How do teachers choose who will teach which topic? It might be that the teacher with the greater expertise (or interest or fondness) about a subject will choose that topic. If the course is team taught again, it might be feasible for teachers to swap topics, having learned from each other when observing in the previous semester.

Cranmer (1999) suggests that one advantage of team teaching is that it makes it possible for the class to be divided into two smaller groups, with one teacher leading each group. However, I would argue that this is more of a parallel experience than a team approach, unless the groups are divided by student ability, so that one teacher has the accelerated students and the other works with the remedial students. Even so, I would suggest that if the class is divided into two groups, then there should be interaction between the groups, such as making presentations to each other or holding a debate, to keep with the spirit of collaborative teaching and learning.

An Intriguing Use of the Team Teaching Concept

One of the most phenomenally exciting examples of online team teaching that I have seen is a class that spanned across the Atlantic and crossed international borders. This course was taught by Gerda Lederer at New School Online University, with another teacher, Albert Lichtblau, and students at the University of Salzburg, Austria. The subject of the course was a study of the Holocaust two generations later. Each American student had an Austrian student partner, and they interviewed friends or relatives alive during World War II, compared experiences and current cultural conditions in their respective countries, and they discussed readings. Both teachers took turns posting information.

Handling an Interruption or Unexpected Change of Direction

Of particular importance in my mind is Cranmer's (1999) point about what should happen in a team teaching situation if there is a sudden interruption or unexpected change of direction in the class, possibly brought about by a student's question or comment. This can be hard enough, perhaps, if teaching solo—though less hard online than on campus, as you have more opportunity for thoughtful reflection or research—but what impact will this have on online team teaching? Assuming the teachers had carefully planned out their lessons and mutually agreed upon who has responsibility for what, then what happens with a sudden lurch in the direction of the course? As we know, there can be a time lag of varying length in online discussions, due to the asynchronicity of the environment, and perhaps this spontaneous change needs to be as quickly addressed as possible.

It would be the democratic and respectful thing to do if the teaching colleagues consulted with each other and arrived at a mutually agreeable new lesson or response. But if the teachers are remote from each other, and logging on from different places, it could take needed time to reach each other, let alone discuss it. So in this case, if the matter is important and urgent enough, the first teacher who sees this spontaneous change should react accordingly to it. This is less likely to occur if you are teaching a hybrid class and you are on the same campus, but that does not stop this type of situation from happening. One instructor might log on while the other is in a long meeting, or away at a conference, or sleeping.

Team Teaching the Hybrid Class

In hybrid classes, I have seen pairs of instructors teach their own separate yet parallel section to their students on campus, and then bring the two sections of students together online to hold particular discussion activities, visit Web sites, and receive online guest speakers. I have also seen hybrids which are team taught both on campus and online. The advantage of the former is that students are in smaller face-to-face groups, which might help opportunities for discussion and involvement, whereas the advantage of the latter is that both teachers are thoroughly familiar to the students, as they are seen in both teaching environments.

Grading

One topic that Cranmer (1999) does not mention in his article is grading, and I found that this was an area of difficulty for me when I team taught. My colleague and I both graded everything, and alas found that we graded very differently. I was generally more generous, and she was less so, so we both needed to reread most papers and spend time coming to a consensus.

Online Testing and Grading

I include testing under the general heading of "Innovative Online Teaching Techniques," as there is always so much students can learn from being tested. We have spoken about students submitting electronic papers, reports, presentations, journals, and short stories, and if a variety of challenging and rigorous learning activities of this nature are given throughout the semester, then the students benefit from frequent feedback and gain a sound idea as to how they are performing in this course. This, in my mind, is true assessment. The word assessment is derived from the Latin root, "to sit next to", and although we do not physically sit next to students when we interact with them online, they can still derive the same benefits of learning if we provide dialogue and feedback.

Knowing a Student's Real Identity

A frequent question about online teaching is how do we know that the students are who they say they are. If you are teaching a hybrid class, this doubt is presumably lessened, because you could give some tests on campus, and thus be present to proctor the exam. But if the class is totally online, or even if it is a hybrid but you want some activities to be tested online, there are many plausible types of online tests.

One important recommendation is to encourage participation in online discussion throughout the semester. This has several advantages. Not only is it beneficial for the student to be an active learner, but also you can grade each student's contribution to discussion. Because of frequently reading student responses throughout the semester, any written reports or essays should not come as a surprise in terms of credibility and authenticity (see Chapter 6, "How to Facilitate and Stimulate Online Discussion").

Grading the Electronic Essay/Take-Home Exam

An electronic paper or essay assignment is similar to a take-home exam. I would recommend that because the student has full access to all online lectures and discussions, as well as the reading materials, it would be of relatively low value to simply test for memorization of facts. This would be a good opportunity to design an examination that stimulates students to think at a very high level when constructing their essay, such as asking them to apply what they know to a different context, or to synthesize their findings, or to provide an overall evaluation, and as such this might help students to reach toward the highest rungs in terms of Bloom's taxonomy.

Ideally, it is best if you do not know which student you are grading. So as not to see the name, it might be best to print the student essays and cover over the names before reading. I think it is beneficial for students to receive their work back from you electronically, once it is graded, because online you have scope to make as many comments as you would like, as the electronic "paper" is infinitely expandable and your remarks always legible (see Chapter 9). You might want to differentiate your remarks from the student's writing by using another color or putting your comments in [brackets]. I avoid writing my comments in capitals, as online this could be construed as shouting. Remember also that critical words can sound harsh and upsetting online, so there is need for encouragement, tact, and suggestions for improvement.

Sometimes it is a good idea to demonstrate to the class, a good student's essay written either in the present class or in a previous one (see Chapter 9), to provide example and encouragement. This would be easy to do online, as you could, with the student author's permission, simply paste it in. Demonstrating the essay online is an easy and efficient way of making this accessible to all students. Some instructors display this model example in a specially created discussion forum, so that after viewing it, students and the instructor hold a discussion in that very forum about the merits of the essay itself, with the essay still visible by scrolling up to it.

Grading for Quality of Responses in Online Discussion

As for grading each student's participation in online discussion, I would recommend that you count qualitative contributions to discussion as a significant percentage of the final grade (see Chapter 6, "How to Facilitate and Stimulate Online Discussion"). Emphasizing quality as opposed to a purely quantitative account of the number of student responses helps to establish to the students that you are interested in how deeply they are considering the issues under discussion, how much they relate the subject matter to their experiences and prior knowledge, and how much their competence in the subject matter is progressing.

If you grade the quality of online discussion responses, it would be wise to let students know how they are doing on an ongoing basis, but be very careful about your timing. If graded too swiftly, they will end the discussion, as students will not see a material benefit in continuing to discuss the topic. If grading comes long after a discussion has reached its natural conclusion, however, the topic is no longer fresh in students' minds, and you will lose the advantage of providing an incentive for students to respond to a topic in a timely fashion or else be penalized in their grade.

Grading Group Work

We now look at how best to grade students based on their group work. Should the group be assessed as a whole, with each group member receiving an identical grade? I would advocate against this. If you were able to observe the group work, you would have derived a definite idea as to how much each student contributed, so it seems that it would be fairer to grade each student accordingly.

Another idea that I have seen used is that the students grade each other's work, and I think this could be a helpful indication, which possibly could be used in conjunction with your own assessment. Jackson (1999), while teaching at New York University, asked students to rank each other according to four dimensions: reliability, participation in group work, intellectual contribution, and contribution to the written project. Students were asked to put these remarks in writing as a private e-mail to him. These dimensions provide concrete measures for grading, rather than being nebulous and impressionistic. Besides this, I believe another clear advantage of asking the students to think about each other's performance is that it helps them with the important process of evaluation and thinking about thinking, termed *metacognition* (see Chapter 3), which is extremely beneficial in advancing knowledge and understanding.

The student grades were then combined with Jackson's own assessment, and resulted in a good reflection of how each student was judged to be doing from a variety of perspectives. Jackson indicated that some students liked this methodology so much that they wrote to him to express their thanks. Although this technique was used with groups of students in the campus class, I believe it would also work well in the online setting. I would also recommend that you take into consideration the feedback from the class to each group's presentation.

Grading Synchronous Online Conversations

There is also the question as to whether each student's participation in synchronous online conversations should be graded. My feeling is that this should not be done in most cases. I say this because unless using techniques such as Brookfield and Preskill's (1999) "Circle of Voices," it generally does not leave room for deep thought and reflection on the topic, as it emphasizes speed above all.

However, if the online chat was used for role-playing, the quality of each student's contribution to the overall virtual play should be graded. This should be combined with how well each student could discuss their performance in terms of the issues it raised, and the quality of responses to other students' questions. Similarly, if the online chat was used for part of the preparatory work contributing to a collaborative group project, then I believe the quality of the final project should be evaluated, as well, perhaps, as weighting the grade according to the participation of each group member in each of the stages of preparation. If the online chat involves interacting with a guest lecturer, it also might be a good idea to grade participation, as this would indicate the degree of preparation each student did beforehand, so as to be ready to ask questions.

I think also it might be a useful exercise to have a student or students synthesize the conversation as viewed in the archived version of the online chat, in terms of extracting the main points of information, and present this on the discussion board. This could count as a graded assignment. Then, as a follow-up exercise, the student could develop this into a further asynchronous discussion or use it as the basis for a research paper. Alternatively, if the class is a hybrid, the student(s) could present the synthesis of the online chat to the campus class, so that the class could continue to discuss the topic further in a face-to-face setting. This would create a good reinforcement of the online chat, provide opportunities for deeper exploration, and help students with different learning styles. It would provide, according to Bloom's taxonomy, opportunities to work at the analytical, synthesis, and even evaluative levels.

Grading Online Multiple-Choice Quizzes

Some instructors like to use online quizzes, and many software programs provide options for creating multiple-choice questions. If opting for multiple-choice tests, much thought needs to go into their design. Some instructors only reach the first level of Bloom's hierarchy in the types of questions they ask, which is recalling facts from memorization. So as to try to make this more rigorous a test, I have seen online instructors do such things as make the multiple-choice test a timed test—something else which many software programs allow you to do—so as to not provide students with sufficient time to look up the answers. This is certainly one method of doing it, but perhaps a test aimed at a higher level of the cognitive hierarchy would be a better and more meaningful way in which to test true learning, rather than giving a timed test for the memorization of facts.

Multiple-choice tests could, for example, be aimed at the comprehension level, instead of the memorization stage. This would assume that the student has the necessary knowledge and information, but now what is required of them is to demonstrate their understanding. Alternatively, the questions could try to determine the student's ability to apply both knowledge and understanding, and this therefore taps into the application level of the hierarchy.

A nice example of a multiple-choice question of application level is as follows (Cameson, et al., 2002):

> Which one of the following memory systems does a piano-tuner mainly use in his occupation?
>
> 1. Echoic memory
> 2. Short-term memory
> 3. Long-term memory
> 4. Mono-auditory memory
> 5. None of the above

It is a question of application, as it tests how to apply the knowledge of memory systems, with the understanding of what each would mean, and it is only when both knowledge and understanding are considered together that the student can chose which is the most applicable for the piano tuner.

Multiple-choice questions can, of course, go beyond testing application to testing analysis, and to be able to truly analyze, the students need the knowledge, the understanding, and the ability to apply to different contexts. Consider the interesting example of a multiple-choice question testing for application. Cameson et al. (2002) provided a table of data of three "mystery" countries arranged in rows, and columns which displayed such economic data as population rate of growth, growth rate of the GNP, and percentages of the population in agriculture, industry, and the service sector. By asking which country is A, B and C, it implies that students must have knowledge of the economic situation in certain countries, that they comprehend the rankings, that they can apply this information, and finally that they are able to successfully analyze it so as to answer the question. This is quite challenging, and as such is a superb test of meaningful student learning.

The highest level of testing, at the evaluation stage, involves testing sophisticated judgments of the interpretation of information. For example, a short piece of writing could be displayed, and the students are then asked if the writing is excellent, good, mediocre, or below average, and each level is clearly defined and specified, so that for example, "excellent" means that explanations are correct and the overall structure is clear, whereas "below average" implies that the explanations are unclear or irrelevant, and the structure is incorrect. By answering this question, students are making judgments according to their knowledge, comprehension, and analysis of the subject matter. In combining these elements, they are making their evaluation based on the specified criteria for each rank.

One word of advice when designing multiple-choice tests; at whatever level your questions are designed to test, be careful in your choice of language. Avoid colloquialisms, which might cause confusion for nonnative English speakers.

In general, you will find that carefully designed multiple-choice questions, aimed at going beyond testing for rote memorization, are a good pedagogical tool. They encourage students to actively think about a subject, and allow them the opportunity to learn from tests.

It is advantageous to make explicit in the syllabus how you will allocate your grades between each of the different learning activities and your expectations of students within each activity. This, I think, relates strongly to the goals and objectives you have set for the course, as an indication of whether these goals are being met, and consequently, whether learning of the subject matter is being advanced. Furthermore, if students can see the range of learning activities at the start of the semester, then hopefully they will know how to pace themselves rather than cramming the night before the work is due.

We have talked in this section about how best to evaluate online students. But what of online education itself? How viable is it? Can meaningful statements be made as to the efficacy of teaching and learning online? These questions will be addressed in the next two chapters.

PART III

ASSESSMENT

At first people refuse to believe that a strange new thing can be done, then they begin to hope it can be done, then they see it can be done—then it is done and all the world wonders why it was not done centuries ago.

—Burnett, F. H., 1911,
The Secret Garden

Recent developments in the socioeconomic climate and in technology have changed ideas about what is important for students to learn. We have become an information economy. Boundaries between jobs are blurring, there is an increase in collaborative teamwork and a need to think and reason effectively in an effort to solve problems. Emphasis is often placed on speed, as information is increasingly being sent electronically, and people must be prepared to think and respond swiftly (National Research Council, 2001).

This points to very significant questions as to whether online education is providing not only a means to a love of learning for its own sake, but also whether it is suitably preparing people for this new work world. Since online education is itself an electronic transfer of information, and since it works best when students are encouraged to work collaboratively and interactively, it would seem that online education could provide the very panacea needed, but let us look into this question more closely. This final section of the book will look at the following:

- Opinions about online teaching and learning
- Building a model of assessment of online education

8

OPINIONS ABOUT ONLINE
TEACHING AND LEARNING

Appearances aren't deceiving, I think,
but you have to know where to look.
—*Smiley, J., 1987, The Age of Grief*

As with any new paradigm shift, there are the naysayers as well as
the enthusiasts. The very same was true at the advent of the printing
press, when it was feared by some that this would mean an end to
Socratic learning. Skepticism and even cynicism about how well an
online class can teach students might develop, especially among those
who feel uncertain about technology. As Kahn (2002) wittily said, "For
a list of all the ways technology has failed to improve the quality of life,
please press three." Below I offer a sprinkling of the types of comments
made either against or in favor of online education.

Online Education Versus Correspondence Courses

Many of us are familiar with David Noble's (1997–2001) criticisms of
online teaching and learning in his series of essays, "Digital Diploma
Mills". Noble, who has studied the history of technology for more than
thirty years, thinks that being called a Luddite is not an insult, as he
believes that technology in teaching is distracting. (The Luddites were
British weavers in the 1800s who fought against technology.) Noble
likens online education to correspondence courses of the early 1900s,
which claimed that they would personalize education, but standards
dropped and eventually the programs failed. A key difference, though,
between correspondence courses and online education, is that whereas
correspondence courses were a one-to-one format, online education is

many to many, thus providing scope for active learning within a highly collaborative framework, and resulting in the discovery of socially constructed meaning. Nevertheless, Noble thinks online learning is doomed because its students and instructors are not able to make use of all five senses, but it has been argued earlier in this book that this might indeed lead to less distractions and greater ability to concentrate purely in the realm of connections of thoughts and concepts.

Caring about Students You Never Meet

Another critic of online education is Carol Fungaroli Sargent, English professor at Georgetown University, who was quoted in the television program, *Sixty Minutes* (2001), as saying, "Education is like sex on the Internet. You can get it online, but it is so much better in person." She thought students were lured online, but that this was an "irresponsible, self-indulgent choice." She seemed to love teaching on campus, feeling that there was a great energy she could see in the classroom when a student was engaged. She asked how could she care about someone she never met in an online class. Furthermore, she had this to say about the hybrid class: "It sounds like the distance-learning camp had to resort to this compromise [hybrid courses] because its ambitions failed miserably." This book has argued that distance does not necessarily impede the excitement of good teaching and learning, and in fact many students have remarked how they felt they knew their instructor and each other better than had been the case in a campus class.

Exerting Quality Control Online

Chancellor Robert Burdall of Berkeley was shown on *Sixty Minutes,* (2001) as saying that he worried about quality control if classes were offered totally online. Arthur Levine, president of Teacher's College at Columbia University, was shown on the same program as thinking that the Internet allows scope for online teaching giants, equivalent to rock stars or athletes, who will be awarded huge sums of money and many other perks as all online universities will be bidding against each other for this superstar.

Overwhelming Aspects of Incorporating Technology

In a 1999 survey at the University of Michigan, Ann Arbor, many faculty members indicated that they wanted one-on-one instruction in using technology, and they wanted this help from someone they knew who was familiar with their work (Lynch, 2002). After all, it takes time to learn how to use technology most effectively, and it is important to make it specific to the needs of the course. As a result, incorporating technology can be understood as being stress inducing and frustrating for some faculty. Along with this is the very real fear for some instructors of a loss of control, as they feel the computer world with its army of instructional designers is intruding into academia. My belief, though, is that if pedagogy remains as the primary focus, and if instructors are trained to learn the basic technology only in as much as it will fulfill the desired pedagogical ends needed for their online courses, then they could take the responsibility of adapting their courses themselves for online delivery and therefore need not be afraid of any intrusions from the technologists.

Many believe, however, that academics are used to being in charge, and enjoy the feeling of power when strolling into a classroom, giving information, and seeing the students rapidly record it in their notebooks. Many professors shy away from technology as they would feel afraid of being in a situation that they do not know, not only in the design of their course, but also in the teaching of it through technological means. They might fear that the students know more than they do, which would mean that they were relinquishing their power (Lynch, 2002). Again, if the role of technology is deemphasized, and if professors are prepared to "give up the chalk" (Patenaude, 1999) so that teaching and learning take place collaboratively rather than hierarchically, then these fears too become unfounded.

Learning to Meaningfully Apply Technology in Education

Larry Cuban, a professor of education at Stanford for the last twenty years, addresses what he feels is "the mostly unfulfilled promise of technology in school reform" (quoted in Carlson, 2001). Cuban, in his book *Oversold and Underused* (2001), looks at the high amounts of spending on technology, yet indicates that it has been largely underutilized as tools in teaching and learning. The thrust of the book is that many teachers and administrators rush to incorporate technology on their campuses, (see Chapter 9, "Technological Stability") as they thought this would make teaching and learning more *efficient*, but Cuban asks, even though technology has reshaped the way business is conducted by promoting greater efficiency, is this a desirable end in education? I would argue that what is of greater importance than efficiency is *effectiveness,* and I believe that online teaching can be very effective if done correctly.

Cuban also found that professors used computers less for teaching than they do in their own home, offices, or library. He says this underuse in the classroom, therefore, is not due to the fact that professors shy away from using them because they are technophobes, but because promoters of technology have little idea of its applied use in teaching. He believes that most software used in education was originally designed for business and it does not translate adequately to meet the very different needs of students and professors.

One Size Does Not Fit All

Along similar lines, one professor at the SUNY Learning Network remarked to me a few years ago, "One size does not fit all," meaning that he thought it was restricting to work within one course template and expect this to suffice for classes on art and design, math, history, or writing, as if this was almost a "cookie-cutter approach." On campus a chemistry lab is necessarily designed differently from an art studio and from a seminar room, so the online environment should better reflect the physical environment of these different types of classes, and the different kinds of activities that go on in each. Whereas I agree with his statement, I do think that most software programs offer a number of options for specific customization, so that courses in different disciplines can in fact look very different from each other.

Hidden Costs

In a fascinating yet controversial book entitled, *Let them Eat Data: How Computers Affect Education, Cultural Diversity, and the Prospects of Ecological Sustainability*, Bowers (2000), looks closely at the consequences of technology on education. He argues that, much as with any form of a progress, there is a double bind, meaning that there are benefits—which are usually talked about extensively—and costs—which are often ignored. As an analogy, Bowers talks of the Industrial Revolution, mentioning that it did indeed advance the wealth and standard of living within society, but it came with costs to the landscape in many areas in the form of blight and pollution, destroyed many individual and self-sufficient cultures, and set the world on the destructive path on which it finds itself today. The same is true, Bowers argues, in the advances in computer technology. We are persuaded through the media, in authoritative and euphoric tones, how marvelous are the latest innovations, so that any criticism is seen as "unwarranted and even subversive" (p. 7). Important questions to ask should be whether these technological advances will make for an "ecologically sustainable and culturally diverse future" (Ibid). Bowers thinks educators have done nothing to look more fully at the consequences of computerization and globalization, as they myopically value technology more than ecological and cultural well-being.

This leads inevitably to questions such as whether, in an attempt to preserve cultural diversity, we should keep our regional academic pockets of education intact, or whether it is advantageous to disperse knowledge and information over as wide an area as possible. Is the spread of information an opportunity or an intrusion? Is the so-called digital divide being widened? As with any new resource, if there are some who benefit and some who lose out, is it fair, based on a cost-benefit analysis, to proceed, thereby penalizing and heightening the relative deprivation of those without? Alternatively, is it fair to deny the spread of online learning, so that those who would have benefited are deprived of that opportunity? What is the most ethical outcome?

My hope is that, similar to the advent of the telephone, there will be an eventual diffusion of computers throughout society. If this will become the case, then it would be beneficial to promote the good of the disadvantaged, rather than deprive the advantaged (Navarro, 2000). Even now, for those students who do not own a computer, they can certainly use the computing facilities of the university (although admittedly, this does not always provide the same convenience and flexibility as possessing one's own computer). Navarro makes an additional and extremely valid point that computers can in fact increase the advantages of some previously disadvantaged groups, such as the old, infirm, or those living in very remote areas. In my experience, it can also provide advantages to those who are constantly mobile. For example, I have had a few touring ballet dancers and actors in some of my online classes, who would log on from their next port of call. As one of them told me, this was not only the perfect way, but also the only way, to complete her education.

To turn one's back on the possibilities of online education because of the opinions of its critics would imply losing out on potentially important opportunities, but at the same time, to paint only a rosy picture would be artificial and misleading. But what do instructors who teach online actually think of their experiences? I think that even though there are some negative aspects, there are indeed many outweighing positives.

Online Teaching Is Time-Consuming

A common complaint about online teaching is how much time it takes. Almeda and Rose (2000), in a survey of satisfaction levels of nine instructors teaching a broad range of topics in fourteen online courses at the University of California Extension, found that some instructors mentioned that length of time was a concern of theirs. Smith, Ferguson, and Caris (2001), in a qualitative study of twenty-one instructors from the SUNY Learning Network, and state universities in California and Indiana, found that instructors said that it can be an extremely lengthy procedure to set up an online class, especially as so much time needs to be devoted to the careful choosing of words to avoid misinterpretation, and the care given to know how best to design the course so that every part of it is in its logically best place. All mentioned having made extensive modifications on the courses they taught on campus, especially in terms of finding ways to motivate students.

Furthermore, once they start teaching the class, the long hours continue. In fact, one study showed that online teaching can take 40 percent more time than teaching in the traditional classroom (Ouellette, 1999). This might be all the more so as it is important for the instructor to be a definite presence in the class, so that the students are reassured that their comments are read and acknowledged (Smith et al., 2001).

I think this points to the need to meaningfully increase the responsibility for students in their own learning process. This decreases the workload on the instructor, and, if done in a variety of exciting ways that meet the needs of many learning styles, can be a terrific educational experience for the students. Ironically, even though it is time consuming, Smith et al. (2001) found that most instructors actually looked forward to their time spent online.

The Value of Being Physically Present

Another difficulty with online teaching, as detected by Smith et al. (2001), is that some instructors did not like being primarily confined to a text-based environment through which to communicate to their students. Some even mentioned that a "life time of teaching skills goes by the wayside. They cannot use their presence and their classroom skills to get their point across. Nor can they use their oral skills to improvise on the spot to deal with behavior problems or educational opportunities" (p. 18). The instructors with whom I have worked, however, have said to the contrary, that they believe that having specific training in online pedagogy has made them thoughtful about teaching and communication in a way that they had not previously been, and that teaching online has actually made them better campus classroom teachers.

Advantages of Freedom and Flexibility

On the positive side of the survey findings, all of the instructors in Almeda and Rose's (2000) study commented that they loved the freedom and flexibility to be anywhere at any time when teaching online. They also mentioned that online teaching appealed to them, as they were interested in professional development to discover new and diverse ways of teaching and presenting innovative learning opportunities.

Richer, More Reflective Discussion

Many instructors in Smith et al.'s (2001) study mentioned the advantage of communication being through the written word, as this tended to enable students to become more reflective, and for learning to become more profound. They also felt that it was more inclusive, as asynchronicity definitely lent a helping hand to those students who might not otherwise contribute to discussion in the campus class. Instructors in Almeda and Rose's (2000) study said that there was generally very strong work from students, as they were "more prepared to stretch themselves online than in the traditional classroom."

Informality as an Online Asset

Interestingly, it was found that instructors thought that the anonymity of all online participants changed the perception of roles, and many students viewed their instructor in a more informal light online, which helped them to better challenge ideas and enable them to engage in a lengthier debate with their instructor than might be feasible on campus. Online classes are not at all alienating, as might be assumed by those unfamiliar with them, but instead are a "labor intensive, highly text-based, intellectually challenging forum which elicits deeper thinking on the part of the students and which presents, for better or worse, more equality between instructor and student" (Smith et al., 2001, p. 19).

High Satisfaction Levels of Online Students and Faculty

In a recent study of the Sloan Consortium, which is a consortium of institutions and organizations committed to quality online education, academics and instructional designers within the group reported that, generally speaking, both student and faculty satisfaction levels were found to be very high for those involved in online education. Many students reported that they had recommended online courses to friends, and that they themselves continued to take online courses. Faculty reported being pleased with online teaching, as they enjoyed this method of teaching with its high degree of interaction, enjoyed easy access to online reference material, and thought online teaching led to effective learning (Sloan, 2002).

These assorted comments about online learning have made me reflect upon a statement of Albert Einstein's, made about half a century ago, and in a totally different context. He said, "It has become appallingly obvious that our technology has far exceeded our humanity." Well, has it? It seems that this view is what has driven most of the arguments against online learning mentioned here. In all likelihood, there are more technological innovations yet to come. Chambers, of CISCO Systems, said on *Sixty Minutes* (2001), in terms of online education, that we have barely even made the first step. Arthur Levine, on the same program, thought that in a matter of ten to fifteen years, it will be feasible to see holograms of the professor and all students there in the room with us as we teach and learn. All of this encompasses enormous implications. Yet, are technology and humanity mutually exclusive? I'd like to think they are definitely not. At all events, I believe that it is crucial to keep in mind that the medium is not the message, but instead is an alternative way of communicating the message, that message being the *content* of what is being taught and learned.

9

BUILDING A MODEL OF ASSESSMENT OF ONLINE EDUCATION

It is the mark of an educated mind to be able to entertain a thought without accepting it.

—Aristotle

The disparate opinions as to the efficacy of online education, shown both by vociferous criticisms and generally favorable attitudinal studies, together with the fact that colleges and universities that offer online courses claim that they are equivalent in terms of credit to their counterpart courses offered on campus, call for a crucial need for a more rigorous and objective assessment of this new type of education to determine what and how much students are learning. Since the very structure of the Internet permits diffusion of its use so rapidly, some academicians might be using online teaching before really knowing how best to do so.

Formative research, which can immediately provide feedback to educators as to how to improve online education, if necessary, is an important first step. Not only is assessment needed for assisting in teaching and learning, but also in evaluating programs and determining how well online teaching and learning, as a new form of education, is faring. Because assessment involves reasoning from evidence, it runs the risk of being slightly imprecise, but this chapter will attempt to offer some alternative views on how assessment can strive to tell the real tale.

Even though online education is, relatively speaking, still in its infancy in terms of the number of years it has been in existence compared to the vast span of human learning, like everything else in the computer world, it has snowballed so rapidly that sufficient online teaching has now occurred for there to be some notion as to its quantitative and qualitative success.

But first let us define what is meant by success. If we define success according to *Webster's New World Dictionary* (1990) as "a favorable result," what exactly does this mean in the context of the virtual classroom? Furthermore, "a favorable result" seems to be a comparative statement. Favorable according to what, and according to whom? As Ehrmann (1995) states, "Unfortunately . . . one can't ask, 'How well is this technology-based approach working, relative to the norm?' since there usually isn't a norm."

Asking the right questions and knowing what to look for in regard to the effectiveness of online teaching is the first important step. It is a rather challenging subject with which to wrestle. Just because an online course is replete with PowerPoint slides, fancy animations, and other flashy displays does not necessarily make it a good course. We are not after a Hollywood production, but should aim to teach a sound, rigorous course through the medium of the Internet, in which student learning flourishes. But even if our primary focus is on teaching and learning, rather than technology, what should we be measuring?

Any of us who have taught online know that it can be good; that we can feel excited, stimulated, challenged, and that we are doing something valuable and viable. We also know that sometimes we feel overwhelmed and frustrated. And we know that many students frequently rave about it, though some have difficulties. But how do emotional reactions translate into specific objective measurements of effectiveness?

Should we be looking, if not at emotional reaction, then at students' grades? Should we be looking at attrition rates? But what does attrition tell us? Unless we interview students who have dropped a course, we might be uncertain as to whether they did so because of some non-course-related impediment in their life or because of this new method of learning. If students dropped at the start of the semester, was it because they were "shopping around" for courses? If we look at grades and attrition rates, should it be a relative measure, as seen in comparison to the class taught solely on campus? Or is it possible to develop an accurate, objective, and specific measurement unique to the online class itself?

Factors to Be Considered when Performing Assessments

Interestingly, in 1978, when a new technical inroad in academia was introduced in the form of teaching by television, McKeachie said, "Unfortunately, there are some hidden traps enthusiasts for one method or another are likely to overlook" (p. 257). Although online education was unheard of then, I would like to apply what McKeachie said about teaching by television to online education, as both represent an important change and both have a profound impact on resultant pedagogy.

Emotional Reactions

McKeachie (1978) wondered whether, if students are taught by "some method quite unusual in their college" (p. 257), which from here on we will interpret for the sake of the present argument as being online teaching, then the very fact that it is new and different might generate excitement; but this might be a reaction to the novelty, and not the educational experience in and of itself. If students in an online course experience tremendous feelings of satisfaction, is it to the detriment of a campus class since it might take more time, and excite students more? Or does it have to be thought of as a balancing act, so that if the scale of satisfaction with online education goes up, the other scale of satisfaction with campus classes plummets? And, still on the basis of emotional reaction, McKeachie points out that some students, rather than feeling excited, might feel angry that they are having to compete with students from the more tried-and-tested *status quo* traditional campus classroom.

What is more, emotional reactions might not only be experienced by students, McKeachie points out, but also by professors. He refers to how, in the face of exciting innovation, so many new professors might briefly enthuse about it, though only a few semesters later their enthusiasm, along with their courses, might wither on the vine. It is for these reasons that I feel that measurements of satisfaction might give some misleading results.

Are All Students Suited to Online Learning?

An important question to ask is, are all students suited to learning online? McKeachie (1978) believes that the students who opt for an innovative approach to their learning are more likely to opt for it again in following semesters than are students who have not yet tried it. I think this is less the case now as far as online learning is concerned, as I have detected some subtle changes in the students I have taught. At first, almost nine years ago when online education was brand new, I think there was a strong process of self-selection among students, meaning that students were generally highly motivated and terrifically enthusiastic. Over time, as more climbed on the bandwagon, I found that as the numbers of students swelled dramatically, the uniform high standard declined. Recently, though, I have noted an increase in bright, motivated students. Of course this is my impression, but if it is objectively true, it makes intuitive sense as first there are the early experimental and adventurous students, then a big wave of students of varying talents and skills, and then, having experienced it, possibly those feeling overwhelmed and unable to perform well when needing to be self-motivated and disciplined, might opt for the campus again. I believe that the ideal online student seems to be a curious mix of independence, in terms of being self-motivated, and also has a definite sense of affiliation and willingness for interaction and collaboration, rather than being a solitary worker.

It is not only caliber that is an issue here, but also lifestyle. Levine, President of Teacher's College at Columbia University, believes that online learning is especially suited to the adult learner, who he says comprises 84 percent of the student body (*Sixty Minutes*, 2001). Increasingly, we see adults returning to college and balancing their jobs and families with educational opportunities. These students, he believes, want the same relationship with their college as they have with their automatic teller machine; namely, great service, convenience, high quality, and even free parking (which, in my mind, amounts to easy access). Although Levine may well be right, I believe there are other not so strictly utilitarian attractions, such as the whole arena of personal attention and human contact missing from his stark comparison with another technological innovation, that of withdrawing money from a "hole in the wall."

As for the undergraduate student who is living on campus, online classes might be very welcome to those who have been typically used to very large lecture halls, as they might benefit from more personal attention online (Navarro, 2000). Hybrids, as opposed to the totally online class, also might provide wonderful opportunities for the discussion from the campus class to spill over online. Students might also enjoy the

diversity of learning opportunities that each medium potentially provides. Lynch (2002) predicts, within about five years, students will come
to expect online classes as a viable alternative from which they would
like to select, and many would come to expect e-books, a 24 × 7 environment, and the possibility of being halfway round the world and still
come to class. However, I do not believe that online education should
ever totally replace campus classes, as most students also benefit from
the face-to-face social interaction that studying on campus provides.

Can Meaningful Comparisons Be Made between Campus and Online Classes?

If indeed there are differences in type and caliber between students who
select a campus class and those who take one online, how then can
comparisons be meaningfully made about the effectiveness of online
education relative to teaching and learning on campus? Might this, in
some sense, be comparing apples and oranges? What does it mean if
it is said that learning effectiveness in the online class is at least as
good if not better than the campus class? Isn't there a wide disparity of
teaching and learning in both environments, online and on campus?
Furthermore, comparative assessments, which can also be called
"norm-referenced," can be informative up to a point, but they are limited as they cannot say how well a student is actually doing in an
absolute sense (National Research Council, 2001). To gain an idea of
how online students perform in absolute terms, this would instead be a
"criterion-referenced" study, such as measuring the ways in which the
students learned the subject and the degree of competence they aquired.

It is impossible to have a control group against which to measure
the success of online teaching. Even if an instructor teaches both in a
campus class and online, the personality and skills of the instructor will
impact on the success of the class. Perhaps what is needed is a large
enough sample of instructors who teach both on campus and online, to
make comparisons and identify trends; but how can we limit for the
personality and communication skills of every individual instructor? It
would seem akin to assuming the purely predictable, robotic, rational
man or woman, whereas we know in reality that human nature does
not work that way.

Furthermore, is it possible to make a blanket statement about the efficacy of online education, since it may vary according to discipline? Are there some subjects that lend themselves better to online education than others? My personal belief is that courses that are most readily suited to online delivery are those that have the most potential for discussion, such as courses in the humanities, social sciences, and writing. If an assessment is made of online education given on one campus or over one university system without distinguishing between academic discipline, can meaningful interpretations be gained?

Impact of the Technology

Another key factor that will impact greatly on relative satisfaction levels of online students is the functionality and usability of the technology itself. Ideally the technology should be seamless and transparent once students become familiar with it. Careful determination should be given by the technical experts when choosing and customizing the software, so that the graphical interface (color, fonts, navigational elements), which affects the way the instructor and students perceive the course on the Web, should be user friendly and pleasingly aesthetic. According to recent government stipulations, access for the student who is vision or hearing impaired should be included (Sonwalker, 2002).

For some students, the following may impede successful learning: unforeseen technical hurdles of accessing the class, finding one's way around the online class, having a computer that keeps crashing, not having a computer at all, or repeatedly receiving error messages and broken links or unclear directions from the instructor leading to ambiguities and uncertainties as to where to click. This points to the need for having a technical support staff who is able to give timely and reliable responses. It also points to how essential it is that the academic institution's server, on which the online classes are housed, operates smoothly, reliably, and with sufficient capacity to avoid delays for each individual user.

Other Possible Frustrations of Online Students

But it is not only technological problems that can lead to frustration. Frustration can also arise if some students do not read all the other student and instructor postings within the online discussion so that it lacks meaningful cohesion, or if some feel overwhelmed by how time consuming it can be, or if some receive insufficient feedback from the instructor so that they are uncertain as to how well they are doing in the class.

Hara and Kling (1999), in their observation of an online class, mentioned that some students felt visual deprivation, stating that if they were on campus, they could tell from body language, a nod of the head, or a smile if they had approval, which is reassuring. This fact highlights the need, mentioned frequently throughout this book, for the online teacher to be supportive, encouraging, and quick to respond. Otherwise student confidence can flag, which is detrimental, because if a class continues to present frustrations for too long, some students might feel stupid in asking questions and become even more lost and frustrated. If a student fails to ask questions or express frustration, an instructor might erroneously assume that all is well in the online class. This is another factor that might therefore skew the accuracy of data on satisfaction levels (Hara and Kling, 1999).

It is vitally important, when conducting an assessment of online education, to be realistic about the possibility of frustration that some students might feel, as it is only when the pitfalls as well as the benefits are taken into account that improvement and progress can be made. Hara and Kling (1999) state that sustained frustration, which might be even more acutely felt when working remotely, can detrimentally affect both a student's cognitive and affective capacities. Cognition can be depleted by frustration as working memory (short term) is distracted, and crucial inferences cannot be made; and students can become far less motivated if frustrations continue.

Is Online Education Suitable for All Instructors?

We also need to ask whether online education is suitable for all instructors, and my feeling is that it is best suited to those instructors who enjoy writing and do it well, who enjoy a Socratic approach to teaching, who personalize education, and who are prepared to spend more time teaching online than they are used to spending in the campus class. Furthermore, it is best suited to instructors who have, or are prepared to develop, a comfort level and competence at using the technology, so that technical frustrations are minimized.

Pragmatic Considerations of Accurately Performing Assessments

One other potential problem of performing assessments that makes intuitive sense is the very act of observation could change the results (McKeachie, 1978). There is also potentially a problem with questionnaire design, as this could introduce an element of bias. Questions may contain words or expressions that are associated with a particular region, and might be especially troublesome in terms of comprehension, given the possible regional and ethnic diversity of students from a global marketplace who are taking an online class (National Research Council, 2001). Even if we were to overlook this point and take various statistical measurements, might we misinterpret the statistical significance of difference?

We also must factor in the extremely large number of variables, as teaching is such a complex process involving interactions between many personalities and the subject matter of the class itself. There is the quality of the curriculum and the nature of the instructional materials to consider, as well as the experiences and skills of the teacher, the support the students receive outside of class, the diversity of the student population, the class size, the opportunities for teachers to work together or to undergo professional development, public opinion, and media coverage (National Research Council, 2001).

So much depends on what is being tested. Some students may find certain tasks difficult whereas others find them easy, even if overall these students are of similar ability. Difference in ability to perform on these tasks could be because of the prior knowledge each student holds (National Research Council, 2001). McKeachie (1978) referred to a stunning study by Parsons, Ketcham, and Beach (1958). This study, which tried to compare the effectiveness of different teaching methods, found that one group of students who did not attend any classes at all, paradoxically performed better on the exam than those who attended class, as the exam itself was based exclusively on the textbook! It was thought that those who attended classes of various types were distracted by other information beyond just the textbook, and so, with cluttered minds, they were less able to focus on questions related to the textbook alone. In this case, it seems that pure memorization and recall of facts were being examined, but as McKeachie (1978) says, ". . . one cannot conclude that a particular method is superior in achieving all goals, if only one outcome has been measured" (p. 260). I agree! If we think back to the six levels of learning indentified by Bloom (1956), reliance on grades can be yet another variable which could muddle a straightforward comparison of effectiveness between online and campus teaching.

Furthermore, grade results might be inaccurate measures of assessment of online education as some students might strive to do well, even if the learning environment is very poor, as they are so motivated by the importance of excellent grades. In other words, they might do independent study to compensate. Even if the totally online course is considered equivalent to the campus class or hybrid class, in terms of the university recognition of the number of credits, can it really be so? Because students are learning in different ways, the exams must reflect this difference in learning and be suited to each learning environment.

Transference of Knowledge and Skills

Looking beyond the immediate education in a particular class to transfer of that knowledge to other classes, as well as to ultimate career success, can it be deduced that online students make more or less use of their knowledge and skills than those who were educated on campus? This is important as education, after all, should not end at the conclusion of the course. Ehrmann (1995), quoting from the findings of Pascarella and Terenzini (1991) in their twenty-year study of the impact of college on students, mentioned that these researchers found virtually no correlation between grades and work achievement for campus students after graduation. Why was this? Was this because of the "stickiness" of preexisting knowledge, even if it is misinformed? Are Pascarella and Terenzini's results an anomaly, or are they generally true? If this had been the case for students educated on campus, is it possible that online students will do much better? Is it possible to say, as some students take hybrid classes, some take a mix of online and campus classes, and some take their degrees entirely online?

A Criteria-Referenced Study: Assessment as a Measure of Achievement of Course Goals and Learning Outcomes

Rather than attempting to do a comparative study between traditional campus teaching and online teaching to assess the efficacy of online education, it would seem that a better approach would be to shift focus to a criteria-referenced study, that concentrates instead on whether the course goals, explicitly stated at the start of the course, have been met by the course's completion, and whether the students have progressed throughout the duration of the course by having meaningfully acquired knowledge. This returns to the true meaning of the word assessment, derived from its Latin root as meaning "to sit next to," with the teacher and student sitting side by side, engaged in continuous and meaningful dialogue and feedback. This technique of investigating whether course goals have been met and of looking at learning outcomes is a method that could accurately assess a course, whether it is taught on campus or online. I would venture to suggest that if this technique is used to assess the efficacy of a course, then elements such as level and quality of participation of each student and visibility of their thinking might become more apparent in the online class than in the campus class.

Not only might it be possible to use this technique to assess a course once it is completed, but also it could be prescriptive in terms of providing indications as to how to intentionally and deliberately construct a course so as to include the following:

- A clear and explicit statement of course goals, along with crisp, logical course structure that enables students to comprehend the requirements of the course. This increases their chances for deep learning to occur, and the course goals to be achieved.
- Discussion questions and techniques that will elicit upper-level thinking and reflection
- A clear reflection of these discussion questions in the grading and assessment

The Flashlight Project, created in the mid 1990s, and directed by Steve Ehrmann, performs important work on assessment of online education. It would be useful to determine how their valid suggestions can be intentionally incorporated into an online course, so as to assess at the end of the semester the extent to which the course goals have been achieved. Ehrmann (1995), believes that the goal for successful online education focuses on selecting "educational strategies for using technology to improve learning outcomes." These educational strategies include:

- Project-based learning
- Collaborative learning
- Learning through repeated revisions of written work
- Improved interaction between and among students and the instructor

Chickering and Ehrmann (1996) applied to the online context the model of "Seven Principles of Good Practice in Undergraduate Education," which was first published in March 1987, as a proposal to improve campus classes. They believed that "[i]f the power of the new technologies is to be fully realized, they should be employed in ways consistent with the Seven Principles." The principles are as follows:

1. Good practice encourages contact between students and faculty
2. Good practice develops reciprocity and cooperation among students
3. Good practice uses active learning techniques
4. Good practice gives prompt feedback
5. Good practice emphasizes time on task
6. Good practice communicates high expectations
7. Good practice respects diverse talents and ways of learning

Let us look at each of these principles in turn and investigate explicitly their implications, both in terms of building specific learning activities into the online course and also in determining learning outcomes and achievement of course goals.

- *Good practice encourages contact between students and faculty:* This implies that knowing a few instructors well greatly helps a student to learn, which might in turn help the student to successfully accomplish the goals of the course. The online class can actually help this to happen in many ways. First, since the online class is always available, it offers the potential for much swifter and more continuous communication than in a class held once or twice a week on campus. Second, if students are dealing with a difficult matter, they might work better by putting it in writing rather than speaking about this. Third, since there is a very definite increase in part-time students and adult learners who have very busy, highly scheduled lives, the online environment offers extended opportunities to contact the instructor, whereas it might have been impossible for these same students to stay after a campus class to talk to the instructor. Fourth, it can help students who are shy, or those from cultures unused to conversing face to face with the instructor, to engage in dialogue, as it offers them time to formulate their response (Chickering and Ehrmann, 1996). Fifth, more intimacy can be developed between all class participants, as working online helps students to ask deeper questions, because they are not being watched and they can become totally absorbed.

This could result in online discussion which is not just formulaic, but sincere, exciting, and insightful. Each student's participation in online discussion is easily apparent, thus providing the instructor with a ready appreciation as to how well each student is learning. As the instructor, it is important to be highly accessible to the student without being overwhelmed, which can be accomplished by letting students know when they can expect to hear from you.

In many online classes that I have taught, students have remarked at the end of the semester that they have come to know me, and each other, much better than had ever been the case for them in campus classes.

- *Good practice develops reciprocity and cooperation among students:* Good learning should be collaborative and social, instead of competitive and isolated (Chickering and Ehrmann, 1996; Wegerif, 1998), as this helps in the meaningful acquisition of knowledge and in achieving the goals of the course. Online discussion is a fantastically useful tool, whereby the sharing of ideas among the group can be readily facilitated. The instructor should avoid answering each student individually, as if playing many simultaneous games of ping-pong, but instead should try to weave together responses from many students, mentioning them each by name and acknowledging their contributions, and pointing out commonalities and differences of perspective among them. This woven tapestry of multiple perspectives can prompt the instructor to ask more questions and move discussion on to a deeper level. The questions asked by the instructor should not be mundane or ask for recall of memorized facts, but instead should be challenging so that they attempt to deepen enquiry and improve the opportunities to actively acquire knowledge.

As well as discussion, there are other online activities that can stimulate reciprocity and collaboration. These can include any form of group work, such as working on case studies or role-playing, as well as giving feedback to presentations, journals, or writing assignments. Online discussions and collaborative online activities of this nature can reach the synthesis and evaluation stages of Bloom's taxonomy.

Along with the instructor asking high-level questions, the tone in which these questions are asked and responses are given is also of utmost importance. By establishing an encouraging, enthusiastic, and supportive setting, the instructor can stimulate interaction and collaboration among the group. This creates conditions for the development of shared multiple perspectives, which can lead to socially constructed meaning (Berge and Muilenburg, 2002; Wegerif, 1998; National Research Council, 2001).

- *Good practice uses active learning techniques:* This principle outlines how good learning is not a spectator sport (Chickering and Ehrmann, 1996), and does not take the view that students are empty vessels waiting passively to be filled with knowledge which they must memorize. This would be the lowest rung of Bloom's taxonomy. Instead, it asserts that the students will enhance their own learning process, and be most likely to accomplish the goals of the course if they are active.

To establish the right conditions in which the students can be active, the instructor needs to ask high-level questions and set challenging tasks, which stimulate the students to reflect upon the topic and to try to connect it to their experiences so that it feels meaningful. The asynchronous nature of online discussions allows time for this reflection and search for relevance to take place. If the students actively participate in online discussions and in all other online learning activities with deliberation and intentionality, and keep the course goals and objectives clearly in mind, it is likely that they will be motivated to perform to a higher level and will as a result retain the material for much longer as it has become more meaningful. It also could be conjectured that the very act of writing out thoughts as opposed to speaking them might further consolidate the acquisition of the student's knowledge and help each student to better retain it.

- *Good practice gives prompt feedback*:   At the start of the class, it is helpful if the instructor can assess the competence and prior knowledge of each student, and then compare this with each student's competence by the end of each course as a way of assessing progress. This would provide a good indication of learning outcomes and the student's ability to achieve the goals of the course. As was discussed in Chapter 3, prior knowledge might either impede or assist in the acquisition of knowledge. As such, it is crucial that students allow their thinking to be visible to the instructor, as in this way the instructor can provide feedback to each student throughout the course and help to guide them accordingly. The online environment provides the mechanism in which thoughts are made visible, in the form of written responses to discussion.

    Feedback to the students is important as it can help them to reflect upon what they have learned and what they still need to know (Chickering and Ehrmann, 1996) and help them with the skills of metacognition in which they can assess themselves and their progress (National Research Council, 2001). Giving feedback online is simple, since there are permanent records of students' work, and easy access to them. One other advantage of giving feedback to a student's online work is that it is an infinitely expandable space, in which instructor comments can be as extensive as needed, rather than being squashed into and around the student's writing on a possibly cramped sheet of paper.

Informative feedback can be helpful, if not inspirational, to many students. Students can more easily do repeated revisions of their work, taking note of each step toward improvement, and thus deepen their learning. Added to this, students can receive feedback from each other as well as from the instructor. Giving feedback draws on the highest level of thinking (evaluation), and incorporating feedback into making overall improvements of the work can lead to synthesis, which is also upper-level thinking. In this way, it can be appreciated that learning activities that encourage feedback can lead to deep learning.

Feedback can also be in the form of acknowledgment (Graham, Cagiltay, Lim, Craner, and Duffy, 2001). Acknowledgment can take the form of the instructor responding to each student by name in online discussions, so that everyone feels included as part of the group. Acknowledgment can also be given in the context of the instructor sending each student an e-mail to confirm receipt of any student assignment sent electronically, and it is tremendously reassuring to students to know that their work has arrived safely.

- *Good practice emphasizes time on task*:   As Chickering and Ehrmann (1996) state, it is important to allocate realistic amounts of time so that effective teaching and learning can occur. Time means something different online than in the campus class, as the online class exists within the more elastic and subjective realm of a virtual dimension (see Chapter 3). This, though, can prove to be advantageous in that it does not call for immediacy; rather, due to its asynchronous nature, students have time to reflect and think deeply about issues before responding.

  The question then becomes that of how the instructor should optimally pace the course, so that students are neither overwhelmed by too much too fast on the one hand, or bored by excessive periods of inactivity on the other. Optimal pacing of the course—along with a variation of stimulating activities that retain students' interest throughout, and a definite presence of the instructor who engenders a personalized, encouraging tone—might help in the ultimate accomplishment of the goals of the course, and for students to move beyond mere memorization to much higher levels of thinking.

The online class can be timesaving in significant ways: it eliminates the need for commuting or parking, it provides easy access to references rather than having to go to a library, and it provides convenience and flexibility for those with busy schedules (Chickering and Ehrmann, 1996). On the other hand, we know that it certainly takes longer to teach and to learn online than in face-to-face classes. But the extended time online provides prolonged opportunities for thought and connection with the material, so that more learning can potentially be accomplished.

Asynchronicity can result sometimes in time lags in conversation topics, which can be frustrating. It is the job of the instructor to stimulate conversation as much as possible, and make it explicit to students that they need to be discussing the same topic at roughly the same time, so that lengthy time lags can be avoided and the excitement and benefits of meaningful interaction can occur.

- *Good practice communicates high expectations*:   It is beneficial for the instructor to develop and post a syllabus at the start of the semester, in which the course goals and expectations are explicitly enumerated. As stated in Chapter 4, it is advantageous to post the syllabus online, as no students can claim to have lost it. Also, it might be helpful at times throughout the semester to paste key points of information from the syllabus into the announcement area, so as to be eye-catching and to refresh students' memories as to what is expected of them.

The higher the expectations, the more likely it is that students will work to a higher level to try to achieve them (Daloz, 1999). Conversely, a course that does not make explicit its expectations, or that lacks challenging or rigorous expectations, could be creating a situation in which students are drifting, rather than feeling motivated or determined to learn deeply and well.

Stated expectations could include such managerial factors as frequency of participation, rules of civility in online discussions, and integrity. Knowledge of an instructor's expectations helps students to strive toward academic excellence. The right degree of challenge should be incorporated into academic questions and tasks, so as to excite and motivate students, but not to be so tough as to create fear in some students (Fardouly, 2001). One way in which fear might be alleviated, and in which inspiration might be given, is if the instructor demonstrates, with the author's permission, exemplary student assignments or responses, either from the present class or from a previous one (Graham et al., 2001). This is easy for the instructor to do as it will involve the simple act of copying and pasting, and it will also be even more easily accessible to the student than if the work was read aloud in a campus class. This ease of accessibility might help the student to better comprehend what was done well in the demonstrated work, and how best to learn from it.

- *Good practice respects diverse talents and ways of learning*: This is crucial, as it shows the fundamental importance of knowing your students. It is not only important to know the students in terms of their background and experiences, but also to be aware of the multiple intelligences that they bring to the learning environment (Gardner, 2000). Gardner drew up many distinct categories of intelligence, as discussed in Chapter 3.

    Much greater accuracy of assessment can be carried out if we watch our students as they are learning throughout the semester to detect their strengths and intelligences, than from a single standardized test at the end of a course. Knowing the students profoundly can be a good guide as to which are the optimal teaching methods to employ. Online teaching should never be canned. Even if you, as instructor, prepare your mini-lectures ahead of delivery, as long as they remain inaccessible to the students until the time they are needed, you can work on customizing them to best fit the learning styles and talents of the students who occupy your class that semester. Maintaining flexibility in teaching style by finding alternatives ways to teach the same content to students of diverse needs and talents is therefore crucial for optimal learning to take place.

    It might be conjectured that students who Gardner (2000) would categorize as having linguistic-verbal, inter- or intrapersonal, or existential intelligence might be very comfortable and learn well in the online environment, whereas students who possess logical-mathematical, visual-spatial, bodily-kinesthetic, musical-rhythmic, and possibly inter- or intra-personal intelligence might learn better in a face-to-face setting.

This is where the hybrid class can provide strength, as it offers a diversity of environments in and of itself. It can allow for the types of hands-on teaching situations in which it is necessary, or beneficial, to meet face to face, such as in demonstrating art, music, math, or movement; and it can allow for those students who find the online class overwhelming, to see their fellow students and instructor in real time. The online component, on the other hand, can help some students who are shy in a face-to-face class, to find their voice online. It can also be beneficial to those who like to reflect and express themselves best through the written word. Different activities can be performed online and on campus, so that these activities reinforce and supplement each other, and online discussion can continue after a campus class or can be used in preparation for the next campus class.

Online education can include many different types of learning activities, and the array will recognize the multiple intelligences and varying learning styles of the diverse group of students. Besides those mentioned in Chapter 7, such as various kinds of group work, journal writing, case studies, presentations, role-playing, debates, online guests, and virtual field trips, this could also include letting students choose their own research projects, within the stipulated guidelines of the course. This would enable students to contribute their unique perspective and learn in a way meaningful to them.

When respect is given to the diversity of multiple intelligences and learning styles, and the teaching is modified accordingly, students can start to become responsible for their own learning, and as such can meaningfully attain profound learning to the highest levels as identified by Bloom's taxonomy.

Technological Stability

We have talked about first deciding upon educational strategies, and then making use of technology to reach the desired ends, namely, achievement of course goals and impressive learning outcomes. But what happens if the technology used to teach the online classes is replaced too frequently? (Cuban, 2001). After all, does there not seem to be a built-in obsolescence with many aspects of technology, and an assumption, as in the commercials of many products, that if it is new, it must be improved?

Ehrmann (2002a) cautions that many academic institutions feel under pressure to purchase the latest technology, so as not to appear to be falling behind, but that this is done at the expense of not necessarily allowing sufficient time to determine whether the previous technology led to benefits of its own, in terms of the accomplishment of stated educational strategies and goals. He argues cogently that more is needed in trying to improve online education than just improved technology. There is a mix of other factors that plays a significant role, such as online faculty development, which allows for the diffusion of new information and course design suggestions among the educators who will be putting this technology to use.

In using technology to improve educational outcomes, it would be beneficial, Ehrmann (2002a) says, to define the educational goals that one wants to pursue, such as improving research skills, collaborative learning and interaction, creativity, and the ability to transfer the knowledge and skills learned within academia to the work world. It would be helpful, knowing these goals, to select one goal that is of particular concern, and determine if there is a technology that might help to improve this situation. If a new technology is selected, it should be chosen so that it is consistent with the progress that is already being made by the existing technologies in the achievement of the stated goals. In this way, a transfer to a new technology should be as smooth and seamless as possible, and education should not be disrupted. Furthermore, once a new technology is selected, it would be important to immediately track how well this system is working, to maintain an accurate report, both of the progress and the pitfalls.

It should be noted that when a change in technologies and software programs occurs, it will be somewhat disruptive, as it will take students and faculty time to become familiar with how to optimally find their way around and manipulate the new system so as to reach desired ends. Special instruction and orientations should be given, both to faculty and students, but even so it will not be until the system has been sufficiently used that it will start to feel familiar, and that effort in using it will shift from the short-term (working) memory into the long-term memory. It is hoped that this will happen as quickly as possible, so that the mind is freed from concentrating on the workings of the technology to being able to focus once again on the course content itself, so that conditions are right for learning to take place.

This is not to imply that new technologies should be shunned, as there are certainly increasing amounts of sophistication and scope in each new technological development, but the choice of whether to adopt a new technology should always be made with the pedagogical goals firmly in mind.

Concluding Comments about Assessment of Online Education

Learning as a Social Process, Impacted by Long-Term Memory

It is important to develop accurate models of assessment, so as to gain as objective a measure as possible about the efficacy of online education. Prior assessment models as applied to traditional classroom teaching are outdated, as now it is better understood that learning is a social process, enhanced by discussion and interaction (Wegerif, 1998). Long-term memory also plays a crucial role in learning, because it is used to reason efficiently about current information and problems (National Research Council, 2001). As stated in Chapter 3, it is important to understand long-term memory to see what students know, how they know it, and how they use that knowledge to answer new questions, solve problems, and learn new information.

The Assessment Triangle

The National Research Council (2001) states that assessment should consist of three crucial and interrelated components, which together comprise the "Assessment Triangle" (p. 44). Although this model was developed for application to face-to-face classes for grade-school students, much can be learned from this and applied to online education. The assessment triangle is as follows:

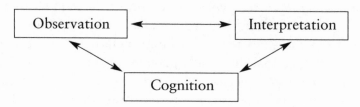

Cognition is the study of how students represent knowledge and develop competence. *Observations* are then made of student performance, and these in turn are *interpreted*, either by statistical or qualitative means. Starting with cognition is what distinguishes the National Research Council's (2001) approach to assessment from other previous studies. As they state: "The methods used in cognitive science to design tasks, observe and analyze cognition, and draw inferences about what a person knows, are applicable to many of the challenges of designing effective educational assessments" (p. 104). This is in keeping with the criteria-referenced model detailed earlier in the chapter, which uses the methodology of the Flashlight Project, in which the starting point is the definition of educational goals and good practices, to design high-level tasks and learning activities, and to draw inferences about learning outcomes and the achievement of these goals.

There is an important relationship between assessment, curriculum, and instruction: The *curriculum* should provide clear views of the course goals and objectives, *assessment* should be performed to detect the present state of the learner in achieving those goals, and *instruction* should be given to close that gap. Instruction should therefore be tailored so as to meet students' needs and talents, and should aim for high-level discussion and suitably challenging tasks, so as to move students toward the highest rung of thinking and learning, as defined by Bloom's taxonomy. Assessment, then, is important not only to determine how well a system is performing, but also as a quest to improve education. It should be measuring how students understand and can explain concepts, how they can reason from what they know and transfer knowledge and skills to other areas, how good they are at solving problems, and how aware they are of their state of knowing so as to be able to self-regulate their learning (National Research Council, 2001).

The Value of Small-Scale Assessments

An important choice to be made is that of scale. Should assessments be broad sweeps at a large scale or should they instead be made at the level of the classroom? Whereas the large-scale approach can lead to public dialogue about the efficacy of online education and policy formation, it is thought that assessments might be most beneficial if made in the classroom. At the local level, cognitive theories can be more easily applied, and changes and improvements can be more readily incorporated, as long as the teacher has had some specific training in knowing how students learn (National Research Council, 2001). For example, as it has been previously argued, grading might be an inaccurate measurement of assessment of the efficacy of online education as it is not necessarily a true measurement of learning. Some students work hard to perfect their performance for a test at the end of the course, yet have learned very little.

What is more important than simple measurements of right or wrong is to attempt, throughout the class, to see how each student is *thinking*. This can become apparent if a student is asked to explain his or her reasoning. The online environment lends itself very well to written responses of explicit lines of reasoning. Once an online student's thinking becomes apparent in this way, the instructor can identify areas of prior knowledge and, should there be any misconceptions, as illustrated by the film, *A Private Universe* (1987) (see Chapter 3), can structure teaching in such a way as to correct them. Alternatively, if the apparent thoughts of the students as written in online discussions reveal solid and correct prior knowledge in this arena, the teacher would be able to reinforce this and help students to expand their knowledge still further, to make more connections, and to build more schema. Furthermore, during the semester, students should be encouraged to develop their skills of metacognition (thinking about thinking), and in this way can identify which areas they feel less confident about, and for which they would like some extra help (National Research Council, 2001).

The Impact on Analytical Skills and Knowledge Acquisition

It would be interesting and important to determine how a student's analytical skills and knowledge acquisition are impacted as a result of being an online learner. In the campus class, the instructor is sometimes faced with the situation of wondering how much time should elapse before a student volunteers to answer a question. Because silence can be uncomfortable and the amount of material to cover is large, the instructor might provide the answer rather than continuing to wait. If so, the instructor does not allow an opportunity for the students to complete active formulation and expression of an answer, nor does the thinking of the students become apparent to that instructor. The online class presents an opportunity for every student to express him or herself, thus giving the instructor the means to know the thinking of all students in the class. This is an advantage over the campus class wherein possibly, because of time constraints and other factors, only the thinking of the dominant students is revealed.

More research needs to be done in this area, but certainly it seems possible that online students, who by the very nature of the learning environment receive information in textual form, process it differently in their long-term memory banks, and have opportunities to make connections and build schema differently than students in a campus class who receive new information through the spoken word. Information communicated online—in contrast to the campus class in which unlistened to words are lost—remains available throughout the duration of the course, thereby increasing the opportunities for continued thought, reflection, and metacognition, since each student can work to some extent at his or her own best pace. Extraneous distractions, such as noise or particular appearances, do not occur in the online class, and lapses of concentration do not mean that the chance of learning a piece of information has vanished, as would be the case in the class on campus. At the same time, though, body language and tone of voice, both of which help in the communication of meaning, are missing online.

Furthermore, possibly the act and increased effort of writing a response in online discussion, as opposed to speaking it aloud in a campus class, makes more of an impact on long-term memory and knowledge acquisition. Additionally, it is often the case that the generally slower act of writing rather than speaking allows time for new ideas, thoughts, and important connections to be made and communicated.

Preconceived Ideas about Innate Ability

What might also prove fascinating to discover is whether students cherish any innate beliefs about their ability to learn well in an online class.

We know that students who hold innate beliefs about being good at a certain subject often do well at it, just as those who have a poor self-image in regard to a discipline often do poorly. This seems to be a case of expected realizations. But since online learning is relatively new, would students have already developed preexisting ideas as to their competence in online classes? Might some students for example, imagine that they would not like an online class, because of fear of technology or a preference to physically be with others rather than working remotely? Might some students imagine they would not be good at online learning as they think they cannot write? This area undoubtedly requires more exploration.

Transference of Acquired Knowledge

It is important to determine whether the previous factors not only impact on an online student's learning in a class currently taken, but also on a student's ability to transfer this knowledge to other classes. In addition, it is important to determine whether online learning creates a lasting impression on long-term memory, so that the knowledge and skills acquired have future applications in terms of careers.

Additional Skills Acquired as an Online Learner

Besides the course content, students in an online class acquire and learn, as a by-product, an important set of skills enabling them to communicate in cyberspace. The first skill is being able to express oneself with clarity in written form, since online classes are text based. It can be conjectured, and indeed I have witnessed among my online students, that writing, just as in any form of exercise, improves the more it is done. This strikes me as very advantageous.

As well as improved writing skills, students also gain the skill of working meaningfully from a remote location, which could impact positively on future possibilities in the workforce, such as telecommuting and conducting online research. Students are also developing skills of effective collaboration and interaction with others, despite the distance. These additional by-product skills yield marvelous benefits, which definitely should be factored in when assessing the efficacy of online education considered over the long term.

The Need for Frequent Formative Assessments and Student Feedback

As for the more immediate situation, it is beneficial for all online instructors to conduct their own assessments throughout the course, especially if they detect difficulties, such as a sudden, drastic decrease in the number of student responses. A single assessment covering many purposes is not necessarily accurate as it contains many compromises. A single assessment at the end of the course is even less useful, as the class is over and therefore there are no opportunities in which to make changes, if needed. Instead, a series of frequent, smaller formative assessments, each of which measure for different factors, could generate a truer picture and lead to improvements in teaching and learning (National Research Council, 2001).

Asking for evaluations from students will help the instructor to avoid making wrong assumptions or misconceptions. Results of the evaluation should be quickly revealed to the students, and any consequent changes speedily implemented. If students realize that what they say in an evaluation might make a difference to the course they are currently in, then they are more likely to provide useful feedback than if the evaluation is executed at the end of the semester. If the evaluation is administered online, then just as with online discussion, students have more time to be reflective and generally write fuller and more helpful comments (Hmieleski and Champagne, 2000).

You could conduct this survey within your online classroom shell, and many software programs allow for anonymous postings which would be of great use in evaluations. Questions to students could be specific if addressing a particular situation, or general, such as in asking them what they like about the course, what most helps them to learn, and if they have any suggestions for improvement. If you are teaching a hybrid, you could also ask students whether the online component meaningfully supplements the rest of the course, and whether any of their suggestions for improvements apply to the campus or online component of the class.

Ehrmann (2000) suggests that you also try to get to the heart of what the students might have to grapple with to work successfully online, as it is important to identify factors that might create obstacles to the possibility of acquiring knowledge and competence. Did all students take the orientation to learn about computer conferencing techniques, do any feel overwhelmed, do they like to collaborate with others in group work, or do they feel it is a waste of time?

Some instructors do not like evaluations, and think that it is in their best interests to keep them as positive as possible, especially as they could signify in decisions about tenure or promotion. Marcus (2001), who teaches creative writing at Columbia, says that many students nowadays have the attitude that they are consumers. He finds that if he genuinely critiques the students' work and includes some negative comments, he runs the risk of receiving poor evaluations from them. Given this, Marcus (2001) admits to employing "dubious teaching techniques," which essentially amount to flattering the students so that they will in turn eventually flatter him in their evaluations. In other words, he concludes, this is a business model in which the customer is always right.

Marcus (2001) asks whether more dissatisfied customers would mean a better learning experience, because honesty and integrity in teaching would be exchanged for flattery. I agree and think that if you involve the students by first asking in the introductory comments what they are hoping to learn from the course, and then conducting assessments throughout the semester, it shifts the emphasis from students being consumers to students being involved participants in their learning process. This should lead to a shared teaching and learning experience, and one that is conducted with integrity.

Feedback from Peers

As instructors, we are part of a larger community of teachers. As such, it is advantageous to discuss with others what went well as a teaching technique, and what was less successful. This can be done as new teachers are being trained to teach online, during the teaching of the course, and at the conclusion of the semester. Peer review can be helpful, in which a team of instructors look at another instructor's online course and then collaboratively offer feedback. This practice is helpful to the instructor of the course being reviewed, and might inform the reviewers of sound and effective techniques that they might want to use in their own courses (McNaught, 2002).

Ultimately, though, to carry out valuable assessments of online education, there should be collaboration between educators, cognitive scientists, curriculum specialists, and psychometricians (National Research Council, 2001). In this way, online instructors could be appropriately trained to know how better to understand how online learning occurs in a social context and also how learning is affected by prior knowledge stored in long-term memory. They could learn techniques whereby to encourage high-level interaction and inclusion of all participants over challenging and rigorous learning activities, as well as learning how to detect what students know and what is their level of competence.

These factors will help to promote conditions in which high-level learning can occur, as reflected by achievement of course goals and learning outcomes, which indicate that students have been thinking at the highest rungs of Bloom's taxonomy. A true collaboration between educators, cognitive scientists, curriculum specialists, and psychometricians would lead to a successful execution of the Assessment Triangle, and thereby help to foster the imperative relationship between curriculum, assessment, and instruction.

AFTERWORD

I believe it is possible for online education to be rigorous, challenging, and comprehensive. However, it is important to realize that to focus exclusively on technology is insufficient when considering including it within one's classes. As Ehrmann (1995) states: "If you are heading in the wrong direction, technology won't help you get to the right place." The primary focus has to be on the teaching, and any decisions should be pedagogically rather than technically driven. It is essential to give thoughtful consideration to explorations of meaningful ways of promoting good teaching and learning through the electronic medium.

Online learning represents a significant paradigm shift in education today. Ouellette (1999) believes that traditional classes have an artificial learning environment as a result of the scheduled times for learning to take place. Online education, in contrast, provides an opportunity for renewal of this paradigm. As stated emphatically by Lynch (2002): "We must also expand our definition of teaching and learning. That calls upon us to open our minds—and our schedules—to asynchronous learning, to the notion that students can learn as well in front of their computers as they do sitting in our lecture halls . . . Appropriate delivery—no less than content—makes a difference."

Lynch (2002) believes that the convenience and flexibility of the online class might well increase learning effectiveness as students log on when they are ready to learn. Learning potential is also increased by interaction and collaboration, as well as by giving students more responsibility for their own learning. Students have greater opportunities for reflection, and a chance to find their own voice (Rohfeld and Hiemstra, 1995). Not only are the pedagogical benefits of online learning there to consider, but also, Lynch states, students today increasingly expect the availability of online educational opportunities.

What is essential for instructors to this endeavor, besides familiarity with the software program, is a sound training on online pedagogy as well as information on how students learn. Then, once the online course is taught, there should be frequent assessments as to how well it is accomplishing its educational goals. Assessments need to be conducted with integrity, so that any areas of difficulty can be noted and suggestions for improvement made. Ehrmann (1995) states: "Without asking hard questions about learning, technology remains an unguided missile." Asking hard questions about learning is exactly what this book has set out to do.

GLOSSARY

Announcement area   The first area the students will see when logging on to the online class; the home page of the class. The announcement area can be used initially to welcome students when they first log on, and thereafter can be used to post informational announcements and reminders throughout the semester.

Asynchronous   Not in real time. The constant availability of the online class throughout the semester means that students and the instructor can log in to the class at a time convenient for them.

Course shell   The empty template of an online course, residing on the Web, which can then be filled with content when it is specifically customized for the purposes of the course.

Discussion board   An online space within the online class, with the capacity to contain separate discussion forums.

Discussion forum   An area, created by the instructor according to topic, in which the instructor and students can interactively post comments, ask questions, and give answers, all as written responses. Each written response clearly displays the author of the response, and the date and time of the posting.

Emoticons   Graphical representations, using keystrokes, to convey emotions.

Graphical interface   The fonts, color, and navigational elements within the online class.

Portfolios   A method by which one can carve up cyberspace, so as to create distinct areas for each student, generally as separate discussion forums, into which each student can post his or her work exclusively, and into which feedback can be given from the students and the instructor.

Real time chat   A feature incorporated within the asynchronous online class, which allows for synchronous online discussions.

Student orientation   A discussion/instruction session prior to the start of the semester, to help students become familiar with the online environment. In this way, students are more prepared to focus on the content of the online class when it begins, rather than feeling confused or stressed about the technology of being online.

Threaded discussion   Used in many online software programs, means that a student or the instructor can post a new idea (thread) as a written response in the online discussion, and then any responses that relate to this initial idea will be arranged such that they lie underneath that response and will be indented by one notch. Thus, threaded discussions lay out discussion strands thematically, instead of chronologically.

URL   A Web address.

Virtual Lounge   The name I have given to the first discussion forum, as an informal space in which all class participants can become acquainted at the start of the semester, and can continue to hold conversations tangential to the course material throughout the duration of the class.

REFERENCES

Almeda, M. B., and K. Rose. 2000. "Instructor Satisfaction in University of California Extension's On-line Writing Curriculum." *Journal of Asynchronous Learning Networks* 4 (3, September).

Anderson, J. A., and M. Adams. 1992. "Acknowledging the Learning Styles of Diverse Student Populations: Implications for Instructional Design." In *Teaching for Diversity: New Directions for Teaching and Learning,* eds. L. Border and N. V. N. Chism. San Francisco: Jossey-Bass, pp. 19–33. http://www.baker.edu/departments/instructech/blended.html

Aristotle 384–322 B.C. Quoted from http://www.quotationspage.com/quotes/Aristotle/

Arnone, M. 2001. "Philosopher's Critique of Online Learning Cites Existentialists (Mostly Dead)." *The Chronicle of Higher Education* (March 15). This article evaluated the book, H. Dreyfus. (2001) *On the Internet (Thinking in Action).* London: Routledge.

Baldwin, R. 2000. "Academic Civility Begins in the Classroom." The Professional & Organizational Development Network in Higher Education. Essays on Teaching Excellence: Towards the Best in the Academy. http://www.cte.umd.edu/

Baum, L. F. [1900] 2000 *The Wonderful Wizard of Oz,* Troll Communications LLC.

BBC Sci/Tech News. 2002. February 22. "Turning into Digital Goldfish." http://news.bbc.co.uk/hi/english/sci/tech/newsid_1834000/1834682.stm

Benson, A., and E. Wright. 1999. "Pedagogy and Policy in the Age of the Wired Professor, *T.H.E. Journal* (November).

Berge, Z., and L. Muilenburg. 2002. March 4. "A Framework for Designing Questions for Online Learning." Berge Collins Associates. http://www.emoderators.com/moderators/muilenburg.html

Blankespoor, H. 1996. "Classroom Atmosphere: A Personal Inventory." In *Inspiring Teaching: Carnegie Professors of the Year Speak,* ed. J. K. Roth. Williston, VT: Anker Publishing Co.

Blum, K. D. 1999. "Gender Differences in Asynchronous Learning in Higher Education: Learning Styles, Participation Barriers and Communication Patterns," *Journal of Asynchronous Learning Networks,* 3 (1, May). http://www.aln.org/alnweb/journal/Vol3_issue1/blum.htm

Boettcher, J. 1999. "What Does Knowledge Look Like and How Can We Help It Grow?" *Syllabus Magazine* (September).

Bowers, C. A. 2000. October. *Let them Eat Data: How Computers Affect Education, Cultural Diversity, and the Prospects of Ecological Sustainability.* Atlanta: University of Georgia Press.

Bromell, N. 2002. "Summa Cum Avaritia." *Harper's Magazine* (February): 74.

Brookfield, S. D., and S. Preskill. 1999. "Getting Discussion Started." Chapter 4 in *Discussion as a Way of Teaching: Tools and Techniques for Democratic Classrooms.* San Fransisco: Jossey-Bass.

Bruce, B. 1998. "Dewey and Technology." *Journal of Adolescent and Adult Literacy* (November). http://www.readingonline.org/electronic/jaal/Nov_column.html

Burnett, F. H. [1911] 1987. *The Secret Garden.* New York: Dell Publishing, p. 267.

Cabell, B. 1999. September 8. "Technological help Lets Students Concentrate on Learning." Cable News Network. http://www.cnn.com/US/9909/08/classroom.2000/

Cameson, J., G. Delpierre, and K. Masters. 2002. "Designing and Managing MCQ's." Appendix C: Bloom's Taxonomy in *University of Leicester, CastleToolkit.* This online handbook is reproduced with permission from the University of Cape Town, South Africa. http://www.le.ac.uk.castle/resources/mcqman/mcqappc.html

Carlson, S. 2001. "Computers Have Had Little Impact in College Classrooms, Stanford U. Professor Argues." *The Chronicle of Higher Education* (November 8).

Carroll, L. [1871] 1997. *Through the looking Glass.* London: Puffin Books.

Carnevale, D. 2001. "A Researcher Says That Professors Should Be Attentive to Students' Approaches to Learning." *The Chronicle of Higher Education* (June 29). http://chronicle.com/free/2001/06/2001062901u.htm

Cassidy, P. S. 2002. "Translating Cultures: Bridging the Next E-Learning Gap." *Educator's Voice* (September 27). http://www.ecollege.com/educator/Resources_edvoice.html

Chickering, A., and S. C. Ehrmann. 1996. "Implementing the Seven Principles: Technology as Lever." *AAHE Bulletin* (October): pp. 3–6.

Chinese Proverbs. Quoted from http://www.quotationpage.com/quotes/Chinese_Proverb/

Cranmer, D. 1999. "Team Teaching." *British Council's Journal,* 10 (April). http://www.britishcouncilpt.org/journal/j1016dc.htm

Crystal, D. 2001. *Language and the Internet*. New York: Cambridge University Press.

Cuban, L. 2001. *Oversold and Underused*. Cambridge, Mass.: Harvard University Press.

Cummings, J. A. 1998. "Promoting Student Interaction in the Virtual College Classroom." http://www.ihets.org/progserv/education/distance/faculty_papers/1998/indiana2.html

Daloz, L. A. 1999. *Mentor: Guiding the Journey of Adult Learners*. San Francisco: Jossey-Bass.

de Bono, E. 1986. *De Bono's Thinking Course*. New York. Facts on File Publications.

Dewey, J. [1938] 1963. *Education and Experience*. New York: Collier Macmillan Publishers.

———. [1910] 1991. "What Is Thought?" Chapter 1 in *How We think*. New York: Prometheus Books, pp. 1–13.

Dewey, John (1859–1952). *The Internet Encyclopedia of Philosophy*. http://www.utm.edu/research/iep/d/dewey.htm

Eastmond, D. 1992. "Effective Facilitation of Computer Conferencing." *Continuing Higher Education Review* 56, pp. 15–20.

Ehrmann, S. C. 1995. "Asking the Right Question: What Does Research Tell Us About Technology and Higher Learning?" *Change: The Magazine of Higher Learning* XXVII (2, March/April): pp. 20–27.

———. 2000. "On the Necessity of Grassroots Evaluation of Educational Technology—Recommendations for Higher Education." *The Technology Source, Michigan Virtual University* (November/December).

———. 2002a. "Improving the Outcome of Higher Education." *Educause* (January/February).

———. 2002b, June. Posting to the AAHEGSIT listserv on stages of faculty development.

Fall, J. 2002. "Teaching With Fun and Humor." *Teacher Help: Article Archive* (January 7). Albuquerque, NM: Wright Group Publishing. http://www.teacherhelp.com/article_archive/classroom_3.html

Fardouly, N. 2001. *Principles of Instructional Design and Adult Learning, How Students Learn*. University of New South Wales, Sydney, Australia. http://www.fbe.unsw.edu.au/learning/instructionaldesign/studentslearn.htm#

Fisher, B. M. 2001. *No Angel in the Classroom: Teaching through Feminist Discourse*. Lanham, Maryland, Md.: Rowman & Littlefield Publishers, Inc.

Galinsky, E. 1999. *Ask the Children: What America's Children Really Think about Working Parents*. New York: William Morrow and Company, Inc.

Gardner, H. 2000. *Intelligence Reframed: Multiple Intelligences for the 21st Century*. New York: Basic Books Publishers.

Graham, C., K. Cagiltay, B. R. Lim, J. Craner, and T. M. Duffy. 2001. "Seven Principles of Effective Teaching: A Practical Lens for Evaluating Online Courses." *Assessment: The Technology Source,* Michigan Virtual University (March/April).
http://ts.mivu.org.default.asp?show=article&id=839

Grassian, E. [1995] 2000. "Thinking Critically about World Wide Web Resources." Regents of the University of California.
http://www.library.ucla.edu/libraries/ college/help/critical/index/htm

Grodney, D. 2001. May 21. Personal e-mail.

Hara, N., and R. Kling. 1999. "Students' Frustrations with a Web-Based Distance Education Course." *First Monday* 4 (12, December).
http://www.firstmonday.dk/issues/issue4_12/hara/index.html

Hmieleski, K., and M. V. Champagne. 2000. "Plugging in to Course Evaluation." *Assessment: The Technology Source,* Michigan Virtual University (September/ October).

Hoover, D. 2002. Personal e-mail.

Hudson, D. 1999. August 18. "Prescription for Learning: Humor in the Classroom. Athens State University, School of Education.
http://hiwaay.net/%7Ekenth/diane/column/p_081899.htm

Hull, K. 2002. Personal e-mail.

Jackson, R. M. 1999. "Developing a Group Grading Strategy including Peer Assessment. *"The Equal Professor, A Forum for Frank Discussion about Teaching at NYU* V (3, April).

Kahn, A. 2000. Quoted in Finch, J., and E. Montambeau, "Beyond Bells and Whistles: Affecting Student Learning through Technology".
http://www.cofc.edu/bellsandwhistles/index.html

Kempster, J. 2002 Interviewed for a colloquy "One Year Later." *The Chronicle of Higher Education* (September 6).

Kolb, D. A. 1984. *Experiential Learning: Experience as the source of Learning and Development.* Englewood Cliffs, N.J.: Prentice Hall.

Kramarae, C. 2001. *The Third Shift: Women Learning Online.* Washington, D.C.: American Association of University Women (AAUW), Educational Foundation Research,
http://www.aauw.org/2000/3rdshift.html. See also, Mayfield, K. 2001. In *Wired Magazine* (September 17).
http://www.wired.com/news/school/0,1383,46689,00.html

Levine, M. 2002. *A Mind at a Time.* New York: Simon and Schuster.

Liu, Y., and D. Ginther. 1999. "Cognitive Styles and Distance Education Online." *Journal of Distance Learning Administration* 2(3).

Lynch, D. 2002. "Professors Should Embrace Technology in Courses." *The Chronicle of Higher Education* (January 18).

Marcus, B. 2001. "Graded by My Students." *Time Magazine* (January 8).

McKeachie, W. J. 1978. "Doing and Evaluating Research on Teaching." Chapter 25 in *Teaching Tips, A Guide for the Beginning College Teacher,* 7th ed. Lexington, Mass.: Heath and Company, pp. 257–263.

———. "Six Roles of Teachers." Chapter 6 in *Teaching Tips,* pp. 68–82.

———. "Personalizing Education." Chapter 24 in *Teaching Tips,* pp. 244–256.

McNaught, C. 2002. "Quality Assurance for Online Courses: Implementing Policy at RMIT." *Assessment: The Technology Source,* Michigan Virtual University (January/February).

Moore, M. G. 1984. "The individual adult learner." In *Adult Learning and Education,* ed. M. Tight. London: Croom Helm, p. 155.

National Research Council. 2001. *Knowing What Students Know: The Science and Design of Educational Assessment.* Washington, D.C.: National Academy Press.

Navarro, P. 2000. "The Promise—and Potential Pitfalls—of Cyberlearning." In *Issues in Web-Based Pedagogy,* ed. R. Cole. Westport, Conn.: Greenwood Press.

Noble, D. 1997–2001. David Noble's Articles on Digital Diploma Mills, Part I–V.
http://www.communication.ucsd.edu/dl/

Ouellette, R. P. 1999. "The Challenge of Distributed Learning as a New Paradigm for Teaching and Learning." University of Maryland University College.
http://polaris.umuc.edu/-rouellet/

Packer, S. 2002. "The Colorblind Cyberclass: Myth and Fact." In *Race in the College Class,* ed. M. Reddy and B. Tusmith. New Brunswick, N.J. Rutgers University Press.

Parsons, T. S., W. A. Ketcham, and L. R. Beach. 1958. "Effects of varying degrees of students interaction and student-teacher contact in college courses." Read at American Sociological Society, August, at Seattle, Washington. (quoted in McKeachie, 1978, p. 260)

Pascarella, E. T., and P. T. Terenzini. 1991. *How College Affects Students. Findings and Insights from Twenty Years of Research.* San Francisco: Jossey-Bass. (quoted in Ehrmann, 1995).

Patenaude, M. 1999. "Keeping them Awake or How I Learned to Relinquish the Spotlight." CCV *Handbook for Basic Writing Instructors.*

Princeton University. 2002. "Academic Integrity at Princeton."
http://www.princeton.edu/pr/pub/integrity/pages/plagiarism.html

Richardson, J., and A. Turner. 2001. "Collaborative Learning in a Virtual Classroom." *National Teaching and Learning Forum Newsletter* 10 (2, February).
http://ntlf.com

Robinson, P. 2000. "Where is Every-Body?" In *Issues in Web-Based Pedagogy,* ed. R. Cole. Westport, Conn.: Greenwood Press.

Rohfeld, R. W., and R. Hiemstra. 1995. "Moderating Discussions in the Electronic Classroom." Berge Collins Associates.
http://www.emoderators.com/ moderators/rohfeld.html
(Originally in *Computer-Mediated Communication and the On-line Classroom in Distance Education*. Creskill, N.J.: Hampton Press).

Russell, B. Quoted from http://www.quotationpage.com/quotes/Bertrand_Russell/11

Ruhleder, K., and M. Twidale. 2000. "Reflective Collaborative Learning on the Web: Drawing on the Masterclass." *First Monday* 5 (5, May).
http://www.firstmonday.dk/issues/issue5_5/ruhleder/

Saba, F., and R. L. Shearer. 1994. "Verifying Key Theoretical Concepts in a Dynamic Model of Distance Education." *The American Journal of Distance Education* 8(1): pp. 36–59.

Salley, R., E. C. Wadsworth, and N. Richardson. 2002. "Tips for Teachers: Encouraging Students in a Racially Diverse Classroom." Derek Bok Center for Teaching and Learning, Harvard.
http://www.fas.harvard.edu/-bok_cen/docs/TFTrace.html

Salmon, G. 2000. *E-Moderating: The Key to Teaching and Learning Online*. London: Kogan Page.

Schneider, A. 1998. "Insubordination and Intimidation Signal the End of Decorum in Many Classrooms." *The Chronicle of Higher Education*.
http://chronicle.com/colloquy/98/rude/background.htm

Schneps, M. H. (producer, director). 1987. *A Private Universe* [film]. Washington, D.C.: The Annenberg/CPB Project. (quoted in Ehrmann, 1995).

Shakespeare, W. Reprinted 1991. Complete Sonnets (Sonnet 16). New York: Dover Publishers.

Shaw, G. B. 1983. *Man and Superman (The Revolutionist's Handbook)*. Harmondsworth, Middlesex: Penguin, p. 260.

Sixty Minutes. CBS. July, 2001.

Sloan Consortium Practices. 2002. http://www.sloan-c.org/effective/index.asp

Smiley, J. [1987] 1989. *The Age of Grief: (A Novella and stories of love, marriage and friendship)*. New York: Ballantine Books, p. 151.

Smith, G. G., D. Ferguson, and M. Caris. 2001. "Teaching College Courses Online vs Face-to-Face." *T.H.E. Journal* (April).

Sonwalker, N. 2002. "A New Methodology for Evaluation: The Pedagogical Rating of Online Courses." *Syllabus Magazine* (January).
http://www.syllabus.com/syllabusmagazine/article.asp?id=5914

Teaching and Educational Development Institute (TEDI). 2002. March. "Tertiary Toolbox: Dealing with Teaching Anxiety." The University of Queensland, Australia.
http://www.tedi.uq.edu.au/teaching/TertiaryToolbox/TeachingAnxiety.html

Turkle, S. 1995. *Life on the Screen; Identity in the Age of the Internet*. New York: Simon and Schuster.

Vella, J. 1997. *Learning to Listen, Learning to Teach.* San Francisco: Jossey-Bass.

Webster's New World Dictionary. 1990. New York: Warner Books.

Wegerif, R. 1998. "The Social Dimension of Asynchronous Learning Networks." *The Journal of Asynchronous Learning Networks* 2 (1, March). http://www.aln.org/alnweb/journal/vol2_issue1/wegerif.htm

Wilson, R. 2002. "Faculty Members Care More about Students, Less about Prestige, Study Finds." *Chronicle of Higher Education* (November).

Wright, F. L. 1932. Quoted from http://www.geocities.com/sotto/1469/flwquote.html

Young, J. R. 2002a. "Logging In With Charles Kerns: Designer of Free Course-Management Software Asks, What Makes a Good Web Site?" *The Chronicle of Higher Education* (January 21). http://web.mit.edu.oki

———. 2002b. "Hybrid Teaching Seeks to End the Divide between Traditional and Online Instruction." *The Chronicle of Higher Education* (March 22).

INDEX